CLASSICAL
MUSIC
WITHOUT
FEAR

CLASSICAL MUSIC WITHOUT FEAR

A Guide for General Audiences

MARIANNE WILLIAMS TOBIAS

Indiana University Press
Bloomington and Indianapolis

This book is a publication of

Indiana University Press
601 North Morton Street
Bloomington, Indiana 47404-3797 USA

http://iupress.indiana.edu

Telephone orders   800-842-6796
Fax orders   812-855-7931
Orders by e-mail   iuporder@indiana.edu

The paper used in this publication meets the minimum requirements
of American National Standard for Information Sciences—Permanence
of Paper for Printed Library Materials, ANSI Z39.48-1984.

Manufactured in the United States of America

Library of Congress Cataloging-in-Publication Data

Tobias, Marianne Williams.
Classical music without fear : a guide for general audiences /
Marianne Williams Tobias.
p. cm.
Includes index.
ISBN 0-253-34277-5 (cloth : alk. paper) — ISBN 0-253-21618-4 (pbk. : alk. paper)
1. Music appreciation. 2. Music—History and criticism. I. Title.
MT90.T52 2003
781.6'8—dc21
2003004104

1 2 3 4 5 08 07 06 05 04 03

We are born into an inheritance,
we are *homo musicus*; defining beauty in
music must therefore entail a definition of
human nature which brings us back to the
humanities and communicativeness.

—Ian McEwan, *Amsterdam*

Domenichino, *St. Cecilia* © Réunion des Musées Nationaux / Art Resource, N.Y.

CONTENTS

Color plates follow page 52.

ACKNOWLEDGMENTS

Classical Music Without Fear is dedicated to the following people.

With respect: to the musicians and staff of the Indianapolis Symphony Orchestra.

With love: to my husband Randy, who has offered steady encouragement and has been a thoughtful, tender, and close partner for this project.

With love: to my children, James and Kathryn, who have been inspiring throughout my life, and who have often and gracefully over many years put aside their plans so there could be time when "Mom could write" or "Mom could practice."

Not a word has been written without the presence of my children and husband in my heart and mind.

With gratitude: to Maestro Raymond Leppard, for insightful critiques of my music notes for many years, graceful patience at all times, for his wit, and for teaching me over and over again the value of high standards in music and in life.

With best wishes: to classical music audiences of today and those yet to come.

Many thanks are due to the following people:

To the wonderful annotators past and present of major American orchestras, whose words have been models of inspiration and instruction.

To Karl Zimmer, who pursued the publication of this book with zeal and determination.

To Geoffrey Lapin and Dinah and Jerry Montgomery: ISO musicians who have, as longtime musical partners, taught me so much about the making of music.

To Andre Watts and Joan Brand: musicians extraordinaire and great friends whose example and loyalty have made deep impact musically and beyond.

To Menahem and Sarah Pressler: inspiring mentor and abiding, wise presences for life and music questions.

To Curt Simic, who engineered and smoothed the way to IU Press.

To Dr. Gayle Sherwood: a brilliant editor and a seasoned scholar, who still, after shepherding this book with its many revisions and saving me from myself, remains a very good friend.

And to the Indianapolis Symphony Orchestra management, which has graciously granted permission and allowed reproduction of program notes and parts thereof, which I have written for them over the past fourteen years.

CLASSICAL
MUSIC
WITHOUT
FEAR

1

GETTING STARTED

Introduction

The title says it all: classical music *can be scary*. The classical music world appears to have an exclusive language and culture. It can seem like a private club whose entry is by invitation only, open only to those who have paid their dues and studied it.

So why bother to understand something that is so intimidating? Why go to a concert where you might not understand the music, not know when to clap, not know what to wear, and so on?

Before you dismiss all classical music, consider the following:

Music is music. Whether it was written yesterday or three hundred years ago, music always uses the same elements: harmony, rhythm, sound, and tunes. Classical music does not contain anything you do not recognize already from popular music. Classical and popular music use the same elements in different ways for the same objective: to entertain, communicate, and inspire.

Experiencing music is part of being human. From ancient times, people have danced, sung, and listened to all different types of music. Today, popular music offers a huge variety: hip-hop, jazz, alternative rock, acid rock, progressive rock, metal, reggae, synthpop, salsa, electronica, movie music, country, western, and rap, to name a few. Classical music has the same variety: not all classical music sounds the same or uses the same instruments. Give it a chance to entertain you, and give yourself a chance to discover a whole new musical world.

How to Use
Classical Music Without Fear

Classical Music Without Fear is written for people who are just starting to learn about classical music or who want to know more. This book addresses your concerns and in easy-to-read sections shows the relevancy of classical music to our lives today. You can use *Classical Music Without Fear* to answer specific questions. The table of contents allows you to choose topics responding to your interest and need without having to read the entire book to find an answer.

The book is organized as follows:

Chapter 1 gives you an idea of what to expect at a concert. What to wear, when to clap, what happens during the concert, what the conductor does, what the major differences are between popular and classical music, and how to find concerts in your area.

Chapter 2 tells you the important facts about the historical periods or *time zones,* explaining some of the larger cultural and philosophical aspects that influenced "classical" music. Each of these time zones summarizes the most significant musical aspects of the period in the "fingerprint" table at the end of each section.

Chapter 3 is a quick and easy guide for reading music. It also explains how to interpret musical scores from various time zones, and how they can tell you something about the music of that period.

Chapter 4 gives you tips on compiling a CD collection and tells you what to listen for in the major works throughout history.

And, if you are not sure about a term, check the glossary section inside the back cover.

Why Will You Like
Classical Music Without Fear?

- It is written for the *intelligent* reader: you are not considered an idiot or a dummy.
- It is a *guide* to enjoying classical music, not a textbook!
- It is written in everyday language.
- It explains the etiquette of classical music for the uninitiated: when to clap, what to wear, why the musicians are dressed up, and what a conductor does.
- It offers some navigational aids to orient you within the music.
- It explains why the classical audience is usually so quiet and the concert hall is dark during a performance.
- It has lots of pictures.

Why pictures? We live in a visual world. We are used to looking at computer screens and televisions. The pictures in the book are selected to show concepts of classical sound. Writing about sound which is always in motion is difficult. Pictures hold still, as do musical scores. That is why pictures and scores are included, to give a visual explanation of the sound of music.

Classical Music Without Fear is about music which is classical, and that means music which has lasted for hundreds of years and will last into the future. It tells you why this special music sounds the way it does, and why there is something in it for you. So give it a try or two, and hopefully you will enjoy the experience.

Why Go to a Concert?

You do not have to go to a classical concert to hear classical music. Frequently it soothes angst at doctors' and dentists' offices, accompanies us while pushing carts down grocery aisles, or adds "classy" ambience while humming to us in elevators or telephone systems. Advertisers for products such as cars to refrigerators to hair dye frequently pitch their wares with classical music crooning in the background. Indeed, you are already "passively acquainted" with more classical music than you might imagine!

On a grander scale, Hollywood often mines classical music to intensify evocative background scores (whether high action or intimate love scenes) for popular movies. Countless varieties of screen hits such as *Dangerous Liaisons, Who Framed Roger Rabbit? Eyes Wide Shut, Driving Miss Daisy, Die Hard, Ace Ventura: Pet Detective,* and *The American President* found just the right accompaniment for screen action in classical repertoire. We were swept into the universe in *2001: A Space Odyssey* with Richard Strauss's tone poem *Thus Spake Zarathustra,* and the award-winning *Runaway Bride* summoned Haydn's Minuet from Sonata no. 33 and Pachelbel's *Canon in D.* Warner Brothers' timeless cartoons are filled with classical background music. Bugs Bunny, Elmer Fudd, and the Road Runner often scamper across the screen accompanied by classical quotes.

Why does Hollywood choose this source? The reason lies far beyond the economic fact that classical repertoire resides in the public domain. Classical music has a connectivity to life—and the living of it—which is unequaled. Existing beyond words and visual stimuli, music— especially classical music—communicates in a voice like no other.

Certain modern convictions about the value of classical music extend beyond entertainment. It has been suspected that, even subliminally, classical music can ratchet up an IQ and "make you smarter." Before birth, babies can now hear a CD such as *Mozart for Mothers-to-Be,* and after birth are treated to the likes of *Baby Needs Beethoven,* while more Mozart snippets hopefully enhance their intellect while drifting into sleep. Nursery schools rock along to *Bibbidi-Bobbidi Bach* and *Heigh-Ho Mozart,* recasting Disney tunes into the style of famous classical composers. For example, "Bella Notte" from *Lady and the Tramp* can be heard in the style of Eric Satie, and "Kiss the Girl" from *The Little Mermaid* can be heard in the style of Sibelius. Primary schools sometimes pump fragments of classical music through loudspeakers at recess, hoping for the magical "Mozart effect."

On the one hand it is good that classical music co-exists with us on a regular, albeit informal basis, such as in stores, commercials, and educational initiatives. On the other hand, when classical music is consistently relegated to a supportive or an atmospheric background, it loses musical impact and status. And, it loses a direct relationship to us. Simply stated, in hearing but not listening, we are deprived of experiencing classical music on its own terms. With that deprivation we are denied its force, beauty, stature, and identity. It was not usually written to *accompany* life's activities. That passive acquaintanceship cannot substitute for the experience and rewards of meeting classical music face to face: in the darkness of a classical concert, where this special music will speak, without distractions, in its original shape, orchestration, and totality.

Sometimes attendance at a classical concert is viewed with apprehension because we are rarely on a "first name basis" with that repertoire. *Classical Music Without Fear* can quickly prepare you to "meet the music" with comprehension and to enjoy the wide range of pieces which have deservedly endured and withstood the test of time . . . and will continue to do so into the future. The variety is endless. There is something for everyone's taste and delight. Sample classical music as you sample food: with curiosity, appetite, and interest. Before long, your individual taste will be defined and satisfied.

Some Encouraging Thoughts

What if you attend a classical concert and don't like it? It is quite possible you will not like some of your visits to classical concerts. That is just fine! You are not expected to like everything—no one does. Remember that classical music is an inheritance which belongs to all of us, and somewhere therein is a legacy for you.

FIGURE 1.2. © Richard Hutchings/CORBIS

To cure a negative classical concert experience, remember these points:

• Classical music for many of us is an acquired taste.
• Just because you did not like one item on your dinner plate does not mean you will quit eating!
• Continue to sample the music with a sense of adventure and patience.

Just because the music is old does not mean it is only for old people. Besides entertainment, classical music speaks to us about life and reactions to it. As humans we share common experiences, whether we lived hundreds of years ago or live today. People, of whatever background or age, have laughed, loved, cried, celebrated, and mourned. Classical music remains uniquely relevant in expressing and touching many sentiments and emotions. It is not surprising that after the tragedy of September 11, 2001, the music we heard most often (Beethoven and Barber, for example) was from the classical repertoire as well as the patriotic. This is music which communicates deeply of life and the living of it. Reflections of life often animate and inspire the enduring music we call classical. It is likely that you will recognize some of your own experiences in that mirror.

In classical music you can find all sorts of specific life topics, such as

- SEX AND LOVE: in works such as *The Miraculous Mandarin, Salome, Petrushka,* and *Romeo and Juliet* settings
- HAVING FUN: in Rossini opera overtures, in Saint-Saëns's zoological fantasy the *Carnival of the Animals,* and throughout celebratory music from all ages
- DEATH AND THE HEREAFTER: in works such as Strauss's *Death and Transfiguration* or *Les préludes* by Liszt
- NATIONAL PRIDE AND PATRIOTISM: in a vast repertoire of music written by composers who wish to express or formulate an explicit national musical voice, such as in *Finlandia* by Sibelius or in the *Russian Easter Overture* of Rimsky-Korsakov, as well as in thousands of works produced by nineteenth- and twentieth-century composers from Eastern Europe, Spain, Mexico, Scandinavia, North America, and Latin America
- STORYTELLING: in the great tone poems and program music of the late nineteenth century, such as *Scheherazade* and *Don Quixote*
- FANTASY AND MYSTERY: in the haunting music of *Symphonie Fantastique* or *Night on Bare Mountain*
- CHILDHOOD AND ITS MEMORIES: in Milhaud's collection *The Baby's Family* and Elgar's *Wand of Youth Suite*
- DANCING: throughout the classical repertoire, in suites, waltzes, symphonies, and ballets from all eras
- TRAVEL ADVENTURES: in works by composers acting as tour guides to foreign lands, such as *Years of Travel* by Liszt, Ravel's *Rapsodie espagnole,* Saint-Saëns's *Egyptian Concerto,* and Tchaikovsky's *Nutcracker Suite*

- POLITICAL STRIFE AND DEFIANCE: roaring through Shostakovich's Fifth Symphony and other musical outcries, such as Beethoven's Overture to *Egmont*
- LITERATURE, POETRY, AND LEGENDS: in many works, such as in Debussy's *Prelude to "The Afternoon of a Faun,"* Schubert songs, Wagner operas, and Rimsky-Korsakov's *The Golden Cockerel,* Sibelius's *Swan of Tuonela,* and Mussorgsky's *Night on Bare Mountain*
- EXPLORATIONS IN SOUND: in the fascinating musical experimentation of the twentieth and twenty-first centuries
- MORALITY, LIFE LESSONS, AND UNIVERSAL PEACE: at the heart of Beethoven's Ninth Symphony and many other profound musical statements, such as Gustav Mahler's *Das Lied von der Erde* and Edward Elgar's *Dream of Gerontius*
- MATH, SCIENCE, TECHNOLOGY, COMPUTERS, AND ROBOTS: performers in the twentieth and twenty-first centuries populate the musical landscape with such pieces as Lejaren Hiller's *Algorithms I, II, and III* (math), and Cage's *Rozart Mix,* which used a complex assortment of tapes
- EMOTIONAL EXUBERANCE: in romantic and modern era works, such as Tchaikovsky's symphonies and Rachmaninoff's concerti
- VISUAL ARTS: in Mussorgsky's *Pictures at an Exhibition,* Martinů's *Frescos of Piero della Franesca,* Rachmaninoff's *Isle of the Dead,* and many more which reflect the famous dictum, "'All art aspires to the condition of music!'"

Finally, a bit of concert insurance. If you can, check the concert program before you go calling the hall or looking up the concert on the Internet. Most orchestras and ensembles have sites which list the repertoire. If the program includes choral works and you do not like singing, don't go! If the program offers all modern works that might sound weird, don't go unless you are feeling adventurous. Look for a concert program which offers a variety of pieces, perhaps also emerging from different time periods, here called *time zones.* A musical buffet is a good beginning.

Remember that you are in charge of your response. Classical music does not dictate your taste. It is not necessary to like everything, and it is quite valid for you to have an opinion right from the beginning.

FIGURE 1.3. ©Hulton-Deutsch Collection/CORBIS

What to Expect at a Classical Music Concert

You are seated by an usher and given a program, which lists the pieces to be played and perhaps includes notes or information about the pieces. The hall is darkened for the performance. This will enable you to listen without distraction. The stage is illumined.

Musicians enter the stage (in no special order) and are seated. The last person to enter is the *concertmaster,* a position established around 1889. This is the *first violinist* seated at the first desk (music stand) to the left of the podium. He or she is greeted with applause, honoring his or her special leadership position in the orchestral family. Concertmasters, called *leaders* in England, have extra duties besides playing. They are like assistants to the conductors. One of the concertmaster's main duties is deciding what bowings the strings should use. Have you ever noticed that the bows go up and down at the same time? The concertmaster has determined those directions, and the musicians have sometimes written the up-bows and down-bows in their scores. This not only coordinates the strings, but is also a great help to the conductor. Another concertmaster duty is to play solo parts within orchestral scores, should there be any.

The orchestra members will then tune their instruments at the concertmaster's direction. A single note is sounded by the oboe (an "A" at 440 vibrations per second). The tuning is organized by sections: first winds and horns, then strings (the concertmaster gives them their own "A"), starting with the lower strings and progressing to the violins. Tuning is a process of matching the established "A" pitch. From this agreed-upon pitch, the orchestra members continue to tune their instruments in relationship to that tone. After the tuning matters are settled, the concertmaster sits down. He or she is the last to be seated, indicating that the orchestra is now ready for the conductor to appear.

A quiet moment follows, and then the conductor enters and is greeted with applause. After acknowledging the applause, he or she mounts the podium and the concert begins.

You will clap after the conclusion of a piece. If the piece has several segments to it, wait until the last segment is completed. These sections are noted in the program. Most of the time in the performance, the musical segments are separated with a pause and you can simply count the sections. If you get lost or are not sure, the safest thing to do is wait until the conductor lays down his or her baton or turns to the audience. Or join the clapping after others have started. See the section "A Typical Concert Program Explained" for more on when to clap (pp. 12–13).

Intermission occurs halfway through the concert. You can remain seated or take a stroll to stretch your legs. You will be summoned back to the concert hall by blinking lobby lights or a fanfare. Intermissions usually last fifteen minutes.

Why are the orchestra members dressed up? Classical musicians usually wear black, with the men in a tuxedo or tails unless it is a special or an informal concert. This formal dress indicates both respect for the music and the occasion, and simply is worn because such dress is traditional. But their dress code does not mean that you must be highly "dressed up" for a classical concert; you can wear

FIGURE 1.4. Conductor, JoAnn Falletta. Photo © Jim Bush. Courtesy of the Buffalo Philharmonic Orchestra.

whatever feels comfortable for you. Tuxedos, tails, and black dresses are "work clothes" for classical orchestra members!

At the conclusion, the conductor, orchestra, and any soloists will receive the opening applause. If there is a soloist, he or she will shake hands with the conductor and possibly the concertmaster as well. At this point it is possible that the conductor will indicate that the orchestra members should rise for applause as well; they will not stand unless invited to do so, in which case they stand briefly and again are seated. The conductor and any soloists usually leave the stage before the applause ends. If the applause continues, they return for more bows. After these are completed, the concertmaster will direct the musicians that it is time for them to leave the stage as well. House-lights are brightened and the concert is over.

One last thing: try not to be late. Because of strict union rules, classical music concerts begin on time. If you are late, it is possible that you will not be seated while the orchestra is playing and will be allowed in only when the first piece is completed. In many modern concert halls, closed circuit television in the lobby will provide you an opportunity to see and to hear what is going on inside. The reason you are not seated is as a courtesy to those who are listening.

Here is a typical program that you might find at a concert:

A Typical Concert Program

| Jean Sibelius, 1865–1957 | Overture to *Karelia*, opus 10 |

Jean Sibelius, 1865–1957   Symphony no. 3 in C Major, opus 52
    Allegro moderato
    Andantino con moto, quasi allegretto
    Moderato-Allegro ma non tanto

Intermission

Johannes Brahms, 1833–97   Concerto in D Major for Violin
and Orchestra, opus 77
    Allegro non troppo
    Adagio
    Allegro giocoso, ma non troppo vivace

A TYPICAL CONCERT PROGRAM EXPLAINED

This program provides you with a large amount of information that will help you enjoy and follow the concert.

The first piece is Sibelius's Overture to *Karlia*, opus 10. The program shows that

1. The composer's name is listed to the left of the piece. In this case, it is Jean Sibelius, a Finnish composer whose dates are 1865–1957.
2. The title indicates that the work is an overture (see glossary).
3. Opus 10 indicates the numbering within the composer's compositions ("opus," or "op.," means "work").
4. There is one movement, since no other words are listed beneath the title. The audience will applaud at the end of this work.

The second piece is another composition by Sibelius, his Symphony no. 3 in C Major, opus 52:

1. The title indicates the piece is a symphony (see glossary).
2. The parts listed below indicate there are three movements or sections. These are "titled" with words which express the tempo (speed) and possibly some additional words which modify the basic instructions. In this case we find

Allegro moderato: at a cheerful but moderate pace
Andantino con moto, quasi allegretto: at a walking pace but with motion, and almost at the speed of an allegro
Moderato-Allegro ma non tanto: the dash indicates that this section has two parts. The first section is to be played at a moderate pace followed by a second section at a cheerful but not too exuberate speed.
The audience will applaud *only* at the end of the final movement, not before.
3. C major indicates the scale or key that the composer selected for this work (see glossary).

After the intermission, the third piece is Brahms's Concerto in D Major for Violin and Orchestra, opus 77:

1. Johannes Brahms was a German composer whose dates are 1833–97.
2. The title indicates the piece is a concerto. There will be a soloist who will stand in front of the orchestra as the "star of the show," and the orchestra will operate in a collaborate, supportive role.
3. The soloist enters with the conductor and there is welcoming applause.
4. There are three parts to the concerto, indicated by the three sections listed.
Allegro non troppo: cheerful but not too fast
Adagio: slow
Allegro giocoso, ma non troppo vivace: cheerfully, but not too fast
Again, the audience will applaud only at the end of the final movement.

Additional Information

Terms indicating the parts of a work are usually written in Italian or German, basic international languages which are used in music.

In the case of certain composers, such as Mozart, the word *opus* is omitted. In its place is another indication, such as the letter "K" in the works of Mozart. These letters refer to the initial of the last name of noted compilers of that composer's works. In Mozart's case, the "K" stands for Ludwig Köchel (also spelled "Koechel"), a compiler of Mozart's compositions. Like the word *opus*, this lettering provides an ordering of the piece within the context of the composer's output. For example, Mozart's Violin Concerto in G Major, K. 216, was written before his String Quartet in B-flat Major, K. 458.

Sometimes musicians refer to a work using only opus numbers or other chronological systems, as in the case of Mozart. If a musician refers to "K. 216," it is immediately understood that the topic is this specific violin concerto. It is possible that you will see the words "major" or "minor" after the letter which refers to the key. This indicates the particular mode (see glossary) of the scale being used.

Unlike most popular music or books that you read, classical music rarely uses unique titles for the different pieces. Instead, classical music pieces are usually identified by generic form (such as symphony or concerto). Hence, recognizing the form will tell you, more or less, what the composer is writing. The firm identity of the piece will be established by its date in terms of a stylistic period (described in chapter 2, "The Time Zones"); its opus number or its chronology is established by someone who organized the composer's works. See "A Typical Concert Program Explained" for examples.

Differences between Classical and Popular Music

The greatest difference between classical and popular music lies in content and behavior. In popular music we usually hear a single tune which stays the same from beginning to end. In classical music the themes (or tunes) are not only presented but *developed*. This developmental process leads the musical ideas into sections of growth and change, revealing the potential within the initial thought to become something greater than the first statement.

These distinctions cited are only for pop music. Jazz resides in a separate category because of its stature in our culture, its content, and its musical sophistication.

Now that you know what to expect from a classical music concert, the experience will be much more relaxing and enjoyable. Check out concerts in your area; a good place to start is by finding a nearby orchestra's homepage on the Internet. Good luck and have fun!

A QUICK GUIDE TO PREPARING FOR A CLASSICAL MUSIC CONCERT

If you are going to a classical concert and wish to "prepare" a bit more, call the hall and ask what the program is going to be. Sometimes programs are also listed on the Internet. For example, if you are attending an Indianapolis Symphony Orchestra concert, go to its website and click on the concert schedule. Then, scroll to the date of your concert.

It is likely that the following genres will be on a classical program. You can read about them by looking up the following explanations and also by referencing the sampler and the glossary (beginning on p. 109 and p. 185), which might include information regarding the exact work being performed.

Concerto or suite written before 1750:
Look up "The Extravagant Baroque" (p. 20)
Read
  • "Concerts and Instrumental Forms of Music" (p. 26)

Oratorio, passion, or cantata:
Look up "The Extravagant Baroque" (p. 20)
Read
  • "Baroque Vocal Productions" (p. 32)

Symphony or concerto written between 1750 and 1820:
Look up "The Cool Classical" (p. 34)
Read
  • Sonata form (p. 40)
  • "The Classical Symphony: A Model for Years to Come" (p. 43)

Symphony or concerto written between 1820 and 1900:
Look up "The Emotional Romantic" (p. 44)
Read
  • "Changes in Musical Form and Behavior" (p. 48)

Symphony or concerto written after 1900:
Look up "The Fragmented Twentieth Century" (p. 58)

Overture, tone poem, divertimento, serenade:
Refer to the glossary

FIGURE 1.5. U2. Photo by Otto Kitsinger/PerformancePhotography.com.

A Comparison of Popular and Classical Music

POPULAR MUSIC

Themes are easy to recall, usually vocal in nature, and short
Repetitious: no development
Single themes predominate
Extramusical effects are common
Lighting: dramatic, invasive, laser beams, etc.
Gyrating performers: extensive body movement
Informal dress
Simple harmonization
Dynamics: loud, heavy amplification
Rhythm: regular and highly accented
Single movement format
Time zone: contemporary or within the past 50 to 60 years
Structures: simple
Homophonic texture
No conductor needed
Lyrics: popular in nature, easily understood
Mass media dissemination
Audience interaction can be loud and frequent
Often geared to the younger generation
Repertoire: primarily American in its roots
Mainstream of culture
Crossover between other popular forms (rock, country)

FIGURE 1.6. Curtis Institute of Music Symphony Orchestra.
The romantic symphony orchestra expanded to include more and more instruments. Here, the wind section includes three bassoons and a contrabassoon.

CLASSICAL MUSIC

Themes are usually instrumental in nature, usually longer than popular themes
Repetition is carefully monitored: variety and development are important
Multiple themes predominate
Darkened concert hall
Rarely employs extramusical effects
Quiet performance demeanor
Usually black formal dress
Richly colored, diverse, and complex harmonization
Dynamics: varied over a wide range; amplification is rare
Rhythm: varied, intricate, nonintrusive
Single or multimovement format
Time zone: hundreds of years as well as current
Structures: often complex, multifaceted; sometimes simple
Polyphonic and homophonic textures
Conductor is needed
Lyrics: if vocal, usually taken from great literature and can be in languages other than English
Not usually presented by mass media
Little or no audience interaction with performers
Multigenerational, tends to appeal to a mature audience
Repertoire: primarily European in its roots
Moved into a subculture status
Crossover to popular music common

THE TIME ZONES

Classical music has been written for hundreds of years. In fact, the term *classical* in its strictest sense applies only to music written over about a sixty-year period! However, *classical* is used in a general sense to mean "enduring" or "lasting." In everyday parlance, the term *classical* extends like an umbrella to cover the vast repertoire of Western art music, irrespective of the time when it was written.

The time periods, or "time zones," in which classical music was written are critically important for your orientation. Composers wrote in the styles of their day, and recognizing the main features of those time zones will help you to prepare for the sounds and the shapes of the music.

This chapter describes the major time zones for you. Bear in mind that the chronological division numbers are arranged for convenience. In practice, new styles emerged in an evolutionary fashion and then matured. Often an old style can be found influencing or running parallel to the new emerging changes.

FIGURE 2.1. Bernini, piazza of St. Peter's. © Howard Davis/
GreatBuildings.com.

The Extravagant Baroque, 1600–1750

The present is loaded with the past and pregnant with the future.

—Gottfried Wilhelm Leibniz, *The Monadology*

You are probably familiar with some of the baroque stars, such as
J. S. Bach, George Frideric Handel, Antonio Vivaldi, Giovanni Gabrieli,
Domenico Scarlatti, and Henry Purcell. Along with these big names
were hundreds of lesser known but talented European composers who
churned out thousands of compositions in the styles and formats
generated by the potent baroque spirit. Within an extraordinary 150
years, musical pioneers at many levels emerged who shaped the destiny
of Western music for succeeding centuries.

In contrast to the control, depersonalization, and serenity marking
Renaissance musical style, the baroque aesthetic embraced exuberance, passion, dynamic contrasts, and an appetite for harmonic and
instrumental color. Poised Renaissance decorum clearly circumscribed

d'esser il migliore dei quattro attivi in Venezia. Vi veniva nominato più tardi Maestro dei concerti e dal 1713 i governatori del pio istituto gli concedevano numerosi congedi per « potersi portare fuori di Venezia per mese uno al impiego delle sue vertuose applicazioni ». Tre anni infatti egli passò a Mantova, verosimilmente dal 1720 al 1723, al servizio del Principe Filippo d'Assia Darmstadt. Nel 1723, dieci anni dopo che Vivaldi rappresentasse a Vicenza la sua prima opera *Ottone in Villa*, seguita dalle rappresentazioni veneziane d'un'altra decina di opere (*Orlando finto pazzo, Arsilda, Costanza trionfante, Tieteberga, Armida, Artabano re dei Parti, ecc.*),

Vivaldi si trovava a Roma e al Teatro Capranica presentava l'*Ercole sul Termodonte*, seguito nel 1724 dal *Giustino* e dalla *Virtù trionfante dell'amore e dell'odio ovvero Tigrane*, in collaborazione con Micheli e Romaldi.

Oltre che compositore, Vivaldi era anche violinista virtuoso, e sempre a Roma ove ebbe l'alto onore di suonare alla presenza del Pontefice, ottenne come tale un caldo successo. Quantz, che era stato a Roma nel '24 poco dopo la partenza del « Prete rosso », scrive : « Ciò che mi giunse all'orecchio di più nuovo fu quel gusto che io ignoravo allora completamente e che si chiamava il gusto lombardo. Vivaldi lo aveva appunto portato a Roma con una delle sue opere che aveva, grazie a questo gusto, soggiogato a tal punto i romani che essi per così dire non sopportavano più ciò che non era concepito in quello stile ». Nel 1725 Vivaldi riprendeva a Venezia la composizione di melodrammi come *Cunegonda, Dorilla*.

A. Vivaldi in una caricatura di Pier Leone Ghezzi.
(*Cod. Vat. Ottoboni* 3114, f. 26).

FIGURE 2.2. Pier Leone Ghezzi, charicature of Antonio Vivaldi. © Bettmann/CORBIS.

such enthusiasms and taste, but the new dramatic musical voice could not be quieted or diverted and would eventually prevail.

Seventeenth-century musical changes were not abruptly enforced. Tendrils of Renaissance style persisted, while the new style operated in a parallel current. During the first part of the baroque period, Western music seesawed between baroque and Renaissance ideas. (These were called the first and second practices.) Ultimately, Western music fully subscribed to the new thinking. In that choice it was fatefully transformed.

What Does *Baroque* Mean?

The term *baroque* (*bah-ROWK*) derived from the Portuguese word *barocco*, meaning an irregularly shaped pearl. In place of the balanced, symmetrical pearl, the oyster produced a stone which was unique, multifaceted, odd, and curious, called a *barocco*. In Italian the word *baroco* was a term for a syllogism used in formal logic to express a wild conclusion. Clearly, neither the conclusion nor the shape was attractive, and this explains the initial pejorative connotation of the word. If something was baroque, it was distorted or overblown and strange. J. J. Rousseau in his *Dictionnaire de Musique* (1798) warned that "Baroque music is that in which the harmony is confused . . . the melody is harsh . . . the intonation difficult . . . and the movement constrained." Obviously, this was not pleasant.

Such negative attributes continued into the nineteenth century but were significantly weakened when challenged in 1888 in Henrich Wolfflin's *Renaissance and Barock*. Wolfflin, focusing on the visual arts, derived a positive conclusion concerning the term. A few years later, Curt Sachs decided that Wolfflin's theory could successfully migrate into music, encapsulated in five tidy categories. In Sachs's view, a direct correlation between the two fields was possible. For example, ornamentation in pictures matched the heavy ornamentation of music. Ultimately Sachs's synchronicity was considered forced and simplistic, and the exact transference of the concept was successfully challenged and refined by later music scholars such as Henry Lang and Manual Bukofzer.

WHAT REMAINED AFTER THE CRITIQUES?

1. The term *baroque* was applied to music written between 1600–1750, with the caveat that those boundaries were relatively fluid.
2. The term *baroque*, even if not very precise, captured dominant features of the prevailing aesthetic.
3. There were indeed certain connections between music and other arts which exemplified the nature and expression of the baroque spirit.

The Baroque Motto: Bigger Is Better!

The baroque savored colossal artistic statements. In painting, the change of scale was dazzling. Huge canvases of painters such as Rembrandt, Velázquez, Rubens, Caravaggio, and Poussin exploded with brilliant colors, vivid contrasts in light and shade, and strong emotions (see plates 1 and 2).

In architecture, enormous churches in cities and extravagant palaces rose from the European landscape, creating impressive statements which, as a subtext, trumpeted the importance and power of the owner or ruler or religion (see fig. 2.1). In Zwiefalten, Germany, a cathedral featured a ceiling painting which extended almost the length of a football field. On the sides of the sanctuary, statues climbed the cathedral walls, reaching into the ceiling. The vision is complex, dramatic, and fascinating, like the *barocco* itself.

Music Takes the Cue

In France and Italy opera was vastly expanded and energized. Extravagant productions could last several hours. Stage sets sometimes soared three stories in height. Singing became emotionally dramatic in the arias (songs), and extra instrumental pieces were sometimes added between acts, adding to the pageantry. Instrumental overtures (pieces which often preceded operas, ballets, suites, etc.) became significant parts of the opera experience. Elaborate special effects were essential features of the spectacles, and exotic machinery was required to create supernatural effects. In one opera, the entire cast was swallowed through trapdoors in the stage while portraying a descent into Hades.

In France, ballet music was also provided for the large ballets which were frequently inserted into the operatic experience. The French royal court loved dancing, and one of Louis XIV's (1643–1715) operas featured the Sun King himself appearing with a crown of sunbeams on his head and light rays shining from his neck, shoulders, and wrists (see plate 4). Costumes as well as stage decor echoed the baroque desire for overwhelming visual impact. Like the overtures, ballets were sometime extracted from operas and performed separately. Contemporary rock concerts have nothing on the shows produced by the baroque in full flight.

Contrast, Emotions, Complexity, and Display

Light and shade in painting provided strong visual contrast. This juxtaposition was called *chiaroscuro*. Sculpture became more elaborate, intricately carved, and emotionally intense. When Bernini placed his marble sculpture *The Ecstasy of St. Theresa* (plate 3) in a presentation niche, he cleverly illumined the work with an unseen window which focused the sun's rays like a spotlight so that the marble shimmered and glowed within the darkness of the church. Music adapted the idea of contrast with successive passages of loud and soft (terraced dynamics), pairings of high and low instruments, and dramatic changes of pace.

Strong emotions were incorporated into music. Increased *chromaticism* (using notes outside the indicated key or scale of the piece) added tension and expressive effects, all serving the desire for a *stilo rappresentativo* which would "stir and penetrate the depths of human feeling." An elaborate system called "the doctrine of affections" (emotions) prescribed a methodology. Basically, the idea of *Affektenlehre,* or theory of affects, derived from Greek doctrines of oratory. In music, the idea of one emotion in a single piece or single section reflected the revival of this antique idea. By the mid–seventeenth century, a host of theorists jumped on the bandwagon and wrote elaborate treatises categorizing emotions and their musical counterparts. Helping the composers along with this procedure was the "theory of musical figures," in which defined standardized musical motifs and behavior communicated specific emotions. As you can see, in its mature state, baroque music was both an elaborate product and process involving intellect as well as inspiration.

Complexity in baroque music can be heard throughout the repertoire, but particularly in the intricate structure of imitative polyphonic pieces such as fugues. In these compositions, several melodic lines are woven together simultaneously in busy-sounding textures. The weaving is controlled by extensive rules involving acceptable combinations and behaviors, and producing a great fugue was a frequent measure of a composer's ability and intellect.

Toccatas, variations, improvisations, and concerti offered special musical vehicles for instrumentalists to display their technique and imagination. Improvisation was a most respected skill, and this procedure is also heard today in jazz performances. Sometimes noble families even sponsored improvisation contests!

An Important New Sound: Monody

If you are singing or listening to a song you focus on a single tune rather than several at one time. This texture is called *monodic*. In the preceding Renaissance period, the simultaneous combinations of many voices (musical lines) had been a standard. In the baroque period, a new idea of one tune at a time was developed. This is known as *monody*.

Important changes were on hand for such musical themes. Melodies were unshackled from matching textual or vocal accents. Once freed from that rhythmic binding, instrumental music gained vital independence. Striking, clear rhythmic patterns (separated from text and speech) were sculpted, propelling melodies with regular, strong pulses.

Providing chordal support for the single melodic line generated new ideas for harmonization. Sometimes an interesting convention called a figured bass was invoked to indicate the chords to be supplied (see fig. 2.3). Numbers indicating chords and their inversions were

FIGURE 2.3. Sample of a baroque figured bass from *Sonata III in A minor* by Henry Purcell.

specified under a single bass line, and the performer was expected to know exactly what those numbers meant in order to "fill in" the notes between the bass and the prominent voice. This convention was a unique musical shorthand, and in its mature state, more than 120 number combinations were to be mastered. Rameau's treatise titled *Traite de l'harmonie* of 1722 was a significant guide and explication of the harmonic practices of those times.

The New Species

Baroque innovations in tuning, tonality, and forms, coupled with a responsive growth in secular music, guaranteed that nothing less than a new species of Western music was being created.

As instrumental music gained independence from vocal inspiration and supportive roles, brighter instruments were needed to "show off" the new thinking. Violins and other stringed instruments, oboes, cornetti, bassoons, trumpets, flutes, organs, and harpsichords marched to the forefront, replacing the more gentle, dispassionate instruments of the Renaissance, such as the lute and viol.

Repertoire for solo instruments and ensembles grew at a phenomenal pace. Concerti, sonatas, and experiments in sinfonias (an ancestor to the symphony) were rapidly spun by composers who found an exciting, fresh outlet for their creativity.

Concerts and Instrumental Forms of Music

Concerts, wherein the audience listened to instrumental music without singing or dancing, became a popular activity. Many of the forms and textures in the classical music you hear today were birthed in the experimentation and formats established in the baroque. From that legacy, four musical forms are particularly relevant for your general instrumental concert experience. These are concerti, suites, fugues, and sonatas.

Concerti

The word *concerto* (*con-CHER-toe*) derives form the Italian verb *concertare,* meaning "to compete," or from the Latin, "to strive or to contend." In either case, the idea invokes the notion of contrast.

In a concerto, the music features a soloist or a small group of soloists playing sometimes separately and sometimes together with a larger ensemble in a *stile concertante* (concerto style). At times, the soloist (or small group) shared thematic subjects with the larger ensemble, and at other times, the soloist presented his own ideas. This contrast of the single or small force against the larger ensemble satisfied the baroque appetite for color and drama, and concerti of many types were written during the period. One of the most popular forms was the concerto grosso, utilizing two groups of instrumentalists (of unequal size and possibly different instruments) in contrasting concerto behavior. Concerto behavior often features alternating emphasis on the soloist or small group and the orchestra and double expositions (orchestra and soloist each having a turn at presenting the main subjects) followed by shared commentary, instrumental dialogue, and independent statements of subsidiary material. The concerto grosso was an important forerunner of the more familiar form of a soloist and an orchestra which we hear today.

Examples of Concerti:

CONCERTI GROSSI

Johann Sebastian Bach: *Brandenberg* Concerti
Antonio Vivaldi: Concerto Grosso in D Minor

CONCERTI FEATURING A SINGLE INSTRUMENT

Ludwig van Beethoven: Piano Concerto no. 3, op. 37; Violin Concerto, op. 61
Franz Liszt: Piano Concerti nos. 1 and 2
Wolfgang Mozart: Piano Concerti K. 537, 467, and 595; Clarinet Concerto, K. 622
Sergey Prokofiev: Piano Concerto no. 1 in D-flat Major
Sergey Rachmaninoff: Piano Concerto no. 2, op. 18
Camille Saint-Saëns: Piano Concerto in G Minor, op. 22
Pyotr Illich Tchaikovsky: Violin Concerto, op. 35
Antonio Vivaldi: Concerto for Flute and Strings no. 2, op. 10

CONCERTI FEATURING MORE THAN ONE INSTRUMENT

Ludwig van Beethoven: Triple Concerto (violin, piano, and cello), op. 56
Johannes Brahms: Concerto for Violin and Cello, op. 102

Wolfgang Mozart: Concerto for Two Pianos, K. 365
Wolfgang Mozart: Sinfonia Concertante for Oboe, Clarinet,
  Bassoon, and Horn, K. 297b
Francis Poulenc: Concerto for Two Pianos in F Minor

CONCERTO FEATURING AN ORCHESTRA

Béla Bartók: Concerto for Orchestra, Sz. 116

Suites

Suites (*sweets*) were a very popular musical form consisting of a
group of dances, usually derived from various national styles. In its
early stages, the suite format was loose (dances were arranged hap-
hazardly), but eventually it was stabilized by a German composer named
Froberger. He disciplined the form into a four-part structure. Following his stabilization, a suite usually opened with the slowly moving
allemande (German), was followed by a rippling courante (French) or
corrente (Italian), which was followed by a stately saraband (Spanish),
and concluded with a fast-paced gigue (English). Obviously a mature
suite was very international in its nature! Sometimes the core instrumental dances were prefaced by an opening prelude, and additional
optional dances (such as minuets or bourrées) were inserted between
the third and fourth parts.

If you see the word *suite* on a concert program, you will hear a
multisegmented work based on a collection of movements of a dancelike nature or origin. There will be pauses between the movements.
Leonard Bernstein's famous *West Side Story Suite* for orchestra is one
of hundreds of instrumental suites which find ancestry in this baroque
concept.

Examples of Suites:

J. S. Bach: *French* Suites, *English* Suites, Four Orchestral Suites
Béla Bartók: *Dance* Suite (1923 version)
Leonard Bernstein: Suite from *West Side Story*
George Handel: *Water Music*
Sergey Rachmaninoff: *Symphonic Dances,* op. 45
Maurice Ravel: *Tombeau de Couperin* (orchestrated in 1919)
Camille Saint-Saëns: *Carnival of the Animals*
Georg Philipp Telemann: Suite in A Minor

Fugues

The baroque fugue (*fewg*) is a monumental musical form and texture. Like fabric, music has texture. The texture is called *thick* if the music sounds heavy or if there are many lines occurring at once, as if many conversations are taking place simultaneously. Any perceived chaos, however, is illusory. Fugal writing is distinctively specialized and has logical behavior and technique lying at the heart of its complex structure. Conversely, if the music sounds less intricate and heavy, the texture is called *thin*. Fugues produce both thick and thin textures in a polyphonic (many-voiced) imitative setting.

How do you know when the music's form is a fugue? Perhaps you remember singing "Row, Row, Row Your Boat," wherein different people or groups start the tune after the initial statement. A fugue relates to that canonic procedure but is far more complicated. Like "Row, Row, Row Your Boat," fugues begin by presenting the main tune in staggered entries, but instead of simply reiterating the first idea, the fugue breeds countersubjects (extensions of the theme or new ideas) which are stacked on top of the ensuing entries. Thus, at the beginning of a fugue, the texture is thin. As the entries compound the scene, the thickness increases (see p. 95 for an example of a fugue).

After all the parts, like people, have entered and stated the tune (called the fugal subject), fugal writing takes advantage of many compositional techniques which truncate or extend the ideas, or flip them upside down, or chop little features or motives from the theme to stir into new compilations. If this is not enough, additional complications can result from episodes interspersed within the statements and partial statements of the main idea. Sometimes these episodes offer a "time out" from fugal momentum, which ultimately always resumes until the close.

Expert baroque composers such as J. S. Bach often demonstrated additional fugal prowess by offering multiple themes at the start, thereby generating successive multiple entries and countersubjects, all braided in an extraordinary aural tapestry. These are called two-, three-, four-, and five-voiced fugues, according to the number of subjects. The process for writing baroque fugues was incredibly complex and governed by intricate, specific rules of fugal combinations and movement to produce acceptable intervallic combinations.

For our purposes, if you hear a lot of musical lines entering and piling up on one another, the music has likely coiled itself into a fugue or a fugato section. Classical, romantic, and modern periods have often featured or referenced fugal style in their works. Fugues were, are, and will always be an irresistible brain game as well as an artistic musical composition and structure.

Examples of fugues:

J. S. Bach: Organ fugue in G Minor; Twenty-four Preludes and
    Fugues for the Well-Tempered Klavier
Benjamin Britten: Young Person's Guide to the Orchestra (Variations and Fugue on a Theme of Purcell)

Sonatas

The Italian verb *sonare* means "to sound." This provided the basis for the term *sonata*. Simply stated, a sonata is a multimovement piece which is sounded (played by a single instrument or a group of instruments) and not sung. A sonata was one of the most fertile and flexible forms initiated in the baroque period. Sonatas for ensembles were sometimes called *sinfonias,* but that terminology was not cast in stone. However, you can easily connect the word *sinfonia* to the word "symphony," the largest iteration of the sonata idea. The elasticity of the form is the secret to its longevity and usefulness from the baroque to this time. Small baroque sinfonias were multimovement works of relatively short duration. By the late nineteenth century, certain symphonies clocked in at over an hour. The incredible sonata idea could easily accommodate both sizes.

The foundational format of sonata form will be most easily discerned by single instrument presentations. Examples of sonatas:

Johannes Brahms: Piano Sonatas
Ludwig van Beethoven: Piano Sonatas
Franz Joseph Haydn: Piano Sonatas
Wolfgang Mozart: Piano Sonatas
Franz Schubert: Piano Sonatas

Where Did They Play All This New Music?

Amid all the sovereign or would-be sovereign states in Europe at that time were many courts of varying sizes and resources. Some boasted their own orchestras, theaters, and possibly resident composers. These were significant venues for the new music. Large cathedrals and churches with fantastic organs were popular concert venues as well. In Venice, the Gabrielis' thrilling concerts in St. Mark's Cathedral were legendary, not only for their music, but also for their novel experimentation in stereophonic sound utilizing two organ lofts in side transepts.

What Happened to Vocal Music?

Vocal music was very significant in the baroque period. Singing embraced and reflected many features of instrumental baroque music. Dramatic presentations, virtuosic display, and expressive singing (both in words and technique, such as the vibrato, which was developed at this time) all found a home in the vast repertoire supplied for opera, oratorios, and other forms of vocal music.

"I was kicked by a horse"

A curious phenomenon in the vocal baroque world was the *castrato* (a castrated male), whose unusual voice was singularly prized. Basically, after castration, males ended up with the voice of a woman in the stronger body of a man. At first these unique singers were used by the church following the admonition in Corinthians, "Let your women keep silence in the churches." Castrati careers also expanded to include opera. One of their selling points was incredible breath control, allowing some castrati to hold a musical line for one or possibly two minutes without taking a breath. For a successful castrato, there was considerable money to be made. According to *The Rough Guide to Classical Music* (edited by Joe Staines), "Such was the allure of the potential income that by the end of the sixteenth century, according to one estimate, some four thousand children were being castrated annually in Italy alone." In their heyday in the eighteenth century, castrati were an essential component of opera, and major singers "commanded astronomical fees."

Mozart wrote parts for them in several works. The most noted of these singers were F. Carlo Broschi, also known as Farinelli, and Haydn's favorite, Senesino. The number of castrati predictably declined as the centuries rolled along. In the end, castrati singing was not a career sought by many. The last professional castrato was Alessandro Moreschi (1858–1921). If you wish to sample his sound, *The Last Castrato* has been digitized from a 1902 gramophone recording. An Italian motion picture, *The Great Farinelli*, in which he was portrayed as sexually active, is another possibility for you as well.

The emasculating operation was usually performed in a bathtub after the castrato-to-be had been rendered unconscious. If the family was poor and could not afford a doctor, the mother just did it herself. Often the castrato would hide this historical truth, explaining his sexual fate by saying he was "kicked by a horse" as a child or had endured a similar catastrophe.

Baroque Vocal Productions:
Operas, Passions, Oratorios, Cantatas

Operas

Italy was the birthplace of baroque opera, which flourished lavishly throughout the period. Around 1603 new music explorations captained by the Florentine Giulio Caccini and his friends in the Florentine Camerata also involved retrospective studies of Greek tragedy and choruses as well as developed the new vocal (monodic) style. Their investigations in part generated one of the most extraordinary genres of Western music: the opera.

Claudio Monteverdi was the most significant composer to first respond to the new musical thinking in opera. His exquisite early operas *Orfeo* (1607) and *Il ritorno d'Ulisse in Patria* (1614) were foundational for the future of opera in the ensuing centuries.

In the mid–seventeenth century, opera was a thriving phenomenon. Venetian opera became an especially popular style, featuring elaborate sets, costumes, virtuosic singing, and consequently heavy reliance on arias. Other countries (excepting France) followed Italy's lead, and Italian-style opera became well known throughout Europe for over a century. Hamburg became the operatic center in Germany, and in 1678 the first public opera house outside of Italy opened its doors there.

Passions

Passions are vocal structures based on biblical narratives, particularly those centering on Christmas or Easter. In the later seventeenth century, the narrative was often paraphrased to fit the musical setting.

Oratorios

The oratorio (meaning place for prayer) is a large-scale work featuring choruses, soloists, and orchestra. A narrator is usually included as well, to explain the development of the story. Like the passion, an oratorio is religious in nature, but does not confine itself to biblical text. George Frideric Handel was a master composer of oratorios, and his *Messiah* is well known in this day as well as in his time. Oratorios were among the most popular vocal expressions of the baroque, and hundreds of composers produced oratorios of varying quality.

Cantatas

Cantatas are multimovement vocal works both of a sacred and secular nature, written on a much smaller scale than oratorios. Like oratorios, cantatas employ soloists, choruses, and instrumental accompaniments. (A workable analogy might be a chamber ensemble as opposed to a large symphony orchestra.) Although composers from Venice published many cantatas in the mid–seventeenth century, Rome was the center of early cantata development and production. The genre grew steadily in popularity throughout the baroque period. J. S. Bach was an expert cantata composer and wrote a total of more than two hundred for every Sunday of the year. One of his most enjoyable secular cantatas is the *Coffee Cantata,* in which every movement describes aspects of coffee!

What Was Happening in Europe Politically during the Baroque?

Music and the other arts were relatively unified under the single banner of the baroque aesthetic, but the political side of Europe presents a highly fragmented, volatile picture. Wars popped up on a regular basis. After the Thirty Years' War (1618–48), Germany alone was shattered into at least three hundred separate states: some historians have assessed there were as many as two thousand, each of which was headed by a "sovereign ruler." Italy presented a similar picture, with political divisions in its city-states and the dominance of the papal state in Rome. France, though not subjected to the fragmentation of Italy and Germany, was internally shaken by civil rebellion in the Fronde uprising and external wars fought under the absolutism of Louis XIV, such as the War of Spanish Succession and the War of the League of Augsburg. To the east, more fragmentation lay in the decaying Holy Roman Empire, filled with differing nationalities which resembled a mini League of Nations. Most of these were yearning to be free. Austria and Prussia in particular, after 1700, came onto the scene as strong disruptive powers.

THE BAROQUE FINGERPRINT

- large-scale, extravagant multimedia works such as operas and ballets
- dramatic contrast and juxtapositions of dynamics (loud and soft)
- one emotion or mood per piece
- complex, dense textures that often use imitation and polyphony
- constant rhythmic propulsion

Baroque composers (see chapter 4, "Classical Music Sampler," for descriptions): J. S. Bach, Handel, Vivaldi

---

The Cool Classical, 1750–1825

Music verily is the mediator between intellectual and sensual life.

—Ludwig van Beethoven, quoted in J. H. N. Sullivan,
Beethoven: His Spiritual Development

In our day, the term *classical music* has been stretched to embrace music which has spanned hundreds of years. It has been convenient to designate *classical music* as a catch-all term for highly divergent yet enduring masterpieces from Bach to the present. There is, however, a more precise meaning for the designation *classical music*. Specifically *classical* music emerged and developed in the classical era of 1750–1825, culminating in the exquisite works of Mozart, Haydn, Beethoven, and Schubert.

As the baroque replaced significant musical styles and forms of the Renaissance, so too did the classical period replace many baroque styles and forms. Like a person, music evolves and changes its personality, its form, and its thinking with the passage of time. After the conclusion of the baroque period in 1750 (the year of J. S. Bach's death), music entered a state of flux and reexamination for about twenty-five years in which new ideas meant to cleanse and delete baroque elements were considered and adopted, leading directly to the forms and sounds we designate as "classical."

Why Did Music Change after 1750?

Significant impetus for musical change came from the philosophy of the Enlightenment, which developed over the course of the eighteenth century. Being a part of life and social context, music reflected aspects of the new philosophy. Enlightenment thinking was skeptical toward tradition but confident in human rationality and in the notion of progress. Old ideas about a personalized, fatherly God were replaced with the idea of God as a "first cause" of the universe. Even God became rational and intellectual. Paris was the heartbeat of the new thinking. The Enlightenment philosophy was trumpeted effectively and loudly by French *philosophes* such as Montesquieu, Rousseau, Buffon, and Voltaire (see fig. 2.4). These men were leaders in a select group called the Encyclopedists, contributors all to the *Encyclopédie,* a seventeen-volume work emerging in 1752 that became the secular bible of the new age. This potent secularism spread enticingly across Europe and America. In revolutionary-era America, Jefferson, Franklin, and the Constitution reflected Enlightenment faith in the capability of man to understand and to control his life. In Europe, Voltaire, Catherine the Great, David Hume, and many others preached the new gospel. Music was profoundly responsive and affected by the social, economic, and cultural changes sweeping across Europe. Like the *philosophes,* music valued and reflected clarity, balance, emotional control, and objectivity. Elegance, poise, and order became not only standards for thinking but also important artistic elements.

FIGURE 2.4.
Jean Baptiste Pigalle,
statue of Voltaire (1694–
1778). Louvre, Paris,
France. © Réunion des
Musès Nationaux/Art
Resource, N.Y.

The selection of 1750, the year of J. S. Bach's death, to separate the baroque from the ensuing rococo and classical eras is symbolic. Bach and Handel had mined the baroque musical aesthetic system and summarized its greatest development and iteration in their work. There was "nothing more to say." However, new ideas had been brewing with those final years, which would influence the upcoming rococo and classical eras. Two of J. S. Bach's sons, C. P. E. Bach and W. F. Bach, emerged as very important post-baroque composers.

Stylistic shifts in music are gradual and evolutionary, not sudden, like turning a light switch on and off. Hints of upcoming changes were in the wind before the baroque cutoff year of 1750.

How to Cool and Trim the
Musical Baroque for Classical Taste? Lose Weight!

Across the board—in texture and concept—the impulse was to shed baroque bulk by thinning textures and simplifying forms. Sim-

FIGURE 2.5. Gardens in Versailles. Photo by Herve Lewandowski.
© Réunion des Musès Nationaux /Art Resource, N.Y.

Notice the clarity, order, and taming of nature represented in
this scene. Nothing is amiss; all is balanced and poised. These
elements are all prominent features of classical music.

plifying would also enhance accessibility. In reaching for this goal,
rococo composers opted for the clarity of monophonic (single-voiced)
music to replace the busy polyphonic textures of baroque. The complexity and thick textures of the past were summarily abandoned.
Melodies were clearly articulated and more symmetrical in shape,
resulting in music which sounded agile, poised, and graceful.

Symmetrical phrases and decorated lines were supported by dis-
creet accompaniment. In place of the extended, long-winded melodic
lines of baroque style, rococo themes were usually tidily harnessed by
four- or eight-measure phrases. Multiple emotions, rather than a single
emotion, could be embraced in a single work, offering a variety of
moods and events, thereby enhancing the goal of "entertainment."
Johann Quantz, an eminent musician and theoretician of those times,
explained, "the old composers were too much absorbed with musical

tricks and carried them too far so that they neglected the essential thing in music which is to move and to please."

Overall these changes created a lightness which was refreshing and important as a conduit to classical style.

The Rococo Bridge to the Classical Period

The reactive quarter-century of approximately 1750–75 was called the rococo. These years spawned several major responses to the past, which influenced and sculpted the distinctive sound and style of classical music. Basically, the new, popular trend intended to cool off the heated complexity and grand scale of the baroque spirit. Like the word *baroque,* the term *rococo* is also borrowed from the sea. *Rococo* is the Italian form of the French word *rocaille,* which is a kind of shell. When we think of a shell we think of a small object with delicate design and coloration, a graceful sculpture. Rococo composers wrote music which conformed to this delicacy and size.

In this regard, particularly influential reactions occurred in France and Germany. In France, the style gallant surfaced, featuring music of consummate elegance, restraint, and poise. In Germany, especially in the court of Frederick the Great and in the works of J. S. Bach's son C. P. E. Bach, the *empfindsamer Stil* (sensitive style) insisted on sentiment and delicately stated emotion. A sensitive style was meant to touch your emotions gently, perhaps to make you wistful instead of tragically despairing. And C. P. E. Bach was on the cutting edge when he wrote important forerunners to the fully developed classical sonata in six important collections "für Kenner und Liebhaber" (for connoisseurs and amateurs).

More classical ideas were peeking out from the works of Sammartini, Boccherini, and J. C. F. and J. C. Bach, two more of J. S. Bach's sons. These new, thinning trends are particularly noticeable in the texture of the music and were successful in erasing baroque intensity and complexity. Instead of generating an overwhelming, impressive, and grand experience, instrumental music found a new personality and a new mission: to be entertaining, graceful, and clear. In the young symphonies and chamber music of the rococo, the music did exactly that.

Gradually, the surface charm of the rococo yielded to the greater vision and power of classical composers. Charm was not enough to carry the day.

The Fusion of Rococo Features and the Development of Mature Classical Music

Empfindsamkeit (sensitive, intimate expression) and the style gallant fused together in the later eighteenth century, the period when classical music (in the strict sense of the term) grew to its finest iteration. Franz Joseph Haydn's life and music bridged the rococo and classical periods.

The potential of sonata form, hinted at in the baroque sinfonias, sonatas, and overtures, was defined and realized in the classical period. This remarkable sonata structure provided both musical logic and a vessel which is still vital.

FIGURE 2.6. François Boucher, *Allegory of Music*
© North Carolina Museum of Art/CORBIS

Classical reliance on and interest in sonata form generated vast quantities of music for solo instruments and orchestras. You will find this form occurring over and over again in the standard music of classical concerts. It is a major genre to consider.

Basically the term sonata form refers primarily to the first movement of a sonata or a classical symphony. Sometimes it is called sonata-allegro form, but in either case, the structure is the same.

Introduction (Optional)	Exposition Main Themes Introduced: Themes 1 and 2	Development Main Themes Developed	Recapitulation Main Themes Reintroduced: Themes 1 and 2	Coda (Optional)
measures 1–40	measures 41–94	measures 94–159	measures 159–201	measures 201–end

FIGURE 2.7. Diagram of sonata form.
Measure numbers from Haydn, Symphony no. 100 (*Military*)
give an indication of the symmetry of classical period sonata form.

Sonata form is tripartite:

Part 1: Exposition. Two contrasting musical ideas (themes) are presented, or "exposed."

Part 2: Development. The two themes are developed. This means that the composer adds new ideas to the basic statement of the theme, imagines different coloration for the themes, or extracts parts of the themes for more examination. Sometimes the two main themes are mixed together and interact.

Part 3: Recapitulation. The two ideas iterated in the opening are recapitulated, meaning they reappear to take a final bow. Sometimes a tiny musical segment called a coda (a tail) is attached at the end to bring the sonata to an extended close.

You will find this form used extensively in classical symphonies and modified slightly for concerti. At times, however, the form is adapted from its theoretical structure described above, but the foundations will remain. You will also find this form adapting to new content when it extends into the romantic period. Its longevity did not stop there, however; sonata form has persisted into the twenty-first century.

Evolution of the Orchestra: A New Sound

In the baroque period, strings held center stage. Classical composers, however, decided that wind instruments could and should be given a more important musical role. Flutes, clarinets (often partnered with horns), and oboes were regarded as capable of carrying and developing melodic ideas, and they gained stature and independence apart from the strings. Brass and horns were also allowed greater participation in thematic presentation, and eventually the more modern orchestra as we know it emerged.

The delicate harpsichord, used frequently in the baroque, totally disappeared from its foundational, pervasive orchestral role. Early pianos developed and provided fatal competition for the harpsichord as a solo instrument. The ability of the piano to sustain tones, to offer graded dynamics (a gradual increase or decrease in sound), and to project a singing tone were features which ousted the tinkling, brittle harpsichord timbre.

The old basso continuo texture completely vanished.

The Vibrant Musical Center: Vienna

Vienna, Austria, became the source and hothouse of the mature classical style. The superstars of the classical composers—Mozart, Haydn, and Beethoven—were all drawn to the atmosphere and the inspiration of that city. Silicon Valley is to computers and software what Vienna was to the development of classical music. Often composers' life spans overlapped, and they were influenced by one another. For a short period, Beethoven took composition lessons from Haydn. Haydn also heard and encouraged the young Mozart. In fact, the coining of the affectionate nickname "Papa Haydn" has been attributed to Mozart.

Where Was This New Music Heard?

The eighteenth century witnessed a profusion of new concert venues. Court life waned in the 1800s, and in that fading, music found a dynamic new audience for orchestral concerts. The aristocracy and nobility still had an important role in supporting musical life, but they were, by default perhaps, joined by the bourgeoisie. Local music societies, comprised both of professionals and amateurs, emerged in cities all across Europe. Their music was heard outside of the courts and the churches in public concerts and in social and political events eagerly attended by the growing bourgeoisie. In many cases these local musical societies evolved into professional ensembles, providing a steady flow of music in their packaged subscription series. Frankfurt, London, Paris, Vienna, Leipzig, Mannheim, and other major cities boasted esteemed musical groups, which played in newly built concert halls, or special "rooms" for music. Significantly, these concerts could be attended by those having the money to purchase a ticket. Music was on its way to becoming democratized and available to many. And composers worked, to a certain degree, in compliance with public taste and the rising middle class.

Popular Influences Enter the Classical Style

Popular taste and culture were influential in musical sound: elements of folk music found their way into the new music; dances such as minuets gained status in the mature symphony structure; and diversionary (just for fun) music emerged in divertimentos and serenades. Certain thrilling features of the new music gave it additional personality. In Mannheim, Germany, the wildly popular "Mannheim rocket" effect was cultivated by leader Johann Stamitz and the Mannheim Orchestra. In Mannheim, musicians were able, through tight control and discipline, to effect a gradual, steady crescendo in themes climbing steadily upward in a fast tempo capped by a dazzling fortissimo (loud) climax which was indeed a rocket that simply "took off." Both the rocket and the "Mannheim sigh"—a kind of melodic tension and release, akin to a human sigh—were signatures of the precise Mannheim Orchestra and the "Mannheim style." Such dramatic effects were pleasing to popular taste and were copied by composers across Europe.

Composers became responsive to their patrons and their public, not just to their personal inspiration. Lighthearted and serious music was frequently written for special events (*pièces d'occasion*) such as a marriage or the investiture of a mayor. One of Mozart's most beautiful symphonies, number 35, was written for the occasion of the ennoblement of a family friend, Siegmund Haffner. Hence it is known as the Haffner Symphony. Likewise, many of Haydn's symphonies and other pieces were written for the enjoyment and special events at the court of the Esterházy family, with whom he lived for thirty years. Both in terms of repertoire and audience, music had bright horizons.

The Classical Symphony:
A Model for Years to Come

When you go to a "classical concert" you will probably hear a symphony. The symphony as we know it was highly developed and polished in the late classical period.

As defined by the classical composers, a classical symphony tended to follow this pattern in four movements:

1. The first movement presented itself in the sonata format described earlier.
2. The second movement was a slower, more pensive contrasting segment, often cast in tripartite ABA form, that is, a theme (A), followed by contrasting material (B), and then the first part recurring again (A). Or the second movement could offer a theme and variations.
3. The third movement was usually a minuet and trio. Like the ABA form, the minuet would present the dance, include a middle contrasting section (called the trio), and then the final section would replay the opening idea, often with some variation.
4. The fourth movement was frequently a rondo, a form similar to a multilayered cake. The rondo theme (the basic part of the cake) would open the movement, a contrasting section would follow (a new layer), the first idea would return (the original cake), a contrasting section (another layer) would follow, and the basic first theme (the original cake) would conclude the movement. In this example, this format can simply be illustrated as ABACA. It was also possible to have more layers of the cake as well, such as ABACADA, and so forth. If this repetition is not clear in the work you hear, it is also possible that you have a hybrid rondo-sonata form, which sometimes occurred as well. Don't worry about following every detail of the form—just enjoy the music!

Patronage and Commissions:
A New Lifestyle for Composers

Although noble and aristocratic patronage of composers continued throughout the classical period, a profoundly influential commercial and economic situation was also at hand. The nobility was no longer the only source of money and support, and the merchant class began to influence and support musical creativity. To earn a living, composers began to write specific works on commission and to write music with an eye to a sale. "What would the London Philharmonic Society be likely to offer me for a symphony?" Beethoven wrote to his pupil and friend Ferdinand Ries in June 1822. Upon receiving the contract, the composer responded, "I accept with pleasure the offer of the London Philharmonic Society [fifty pounds], even though the honorarium from Englishmen cannot meet that of other nations." This "deal" provided the commercial backing for the great Ninth Symphony! For this reason, the Ninth Symphony was first titled "Symphony for England" and was dedicated to the sponsoring society. Later it was rededicated to the king of Prussia. Along with commissions, composers earned income through the music publishing profession. Composers would sell their manuscripts to the publishers, and then these publishing firms disseminated music widely to various orchestras for a fee. Composers were usually not good businessmen, and sometimes they were known to give "first rights" to several publishers simultaneously or in short succession, causing colorful lawsuits and fury.

The Emotional Romantic, 1810–1900

> Music is the only Sensual Pleasure without vice.
>
> —Samuel Johnson, *Johnson Miscellanies*

Countercurrents to the order and disciplined elegance of classical style began to flow in tiny streams during the first quarter of the nineteenth century. Gradually these rivulets formed a river of explosive philosophies and emotions, sweeping away the objectivity, equilibrium, and content of classical style. At the heart of this nineteenth-century phenomenon lay valued notions of personalization, impulsive emotional display, baring the soul, and attraction for the exotic, the mysterious, the enchanting, the fantastic, and the natural. However, nature was no longer exemplified by the benign, tamed world of well-manicured gardens but was viewed as a wild and dangerous yet beguiling force.

THE CLASSICAL FINGERPRINT

- use of sonata form
- clarity of melodic line: a single voice or theme was balanced over chords rather than competing with or intertwined with other themes; themes tended to be shorter than in the baroque period
- harmonic simplicity and formal impact of harmonic function: in place of harmonies generated by the intersection of melodic lines, composers began to support melodies with block chords. Key changes and harmony (generated by the chords) were very important indicators of the shape of the piece and served not only to color the melodic line but also to orient the listener to the musical form.
- extensive repertoire development of chamber music, string quartets, and orchestral symphonies
- dynamic gradation rather than sudden shifts from loud to soft: the terraced dynamics of the baroque were eliminated for the most part
- variety of rhythmic patterns in place of baroque motoric rhythms, spinning on indefinitely. In classical music, rhythms blend neatly one to another and offer a pleasing variety.
- multiple emotions and themes appeared in a single work.

Classical composers (see chapter 4, "Classical Music Sampler" for descriptions): Beethoven (earlier works), Haydn, Mozart, Schubert

Enlightenment confidence in human intellect yielded to a belief that emotion and instinct were not only of value but were also sources of truth. Well-behaved paintings of the eighteenth century gave way to canvases such as those of Delacroix, which reflected a world filled with supernatural, magical, imaginative freedom and mystery. Literary masterpieces generated by poets such as Byron, Schiller, and Goethe and novelists such as Walter Scott reflected romantic enthusiasms and tastes.

Music responded to these stirring ideas by breaking classical formal constraints and allowing lavish, unrestrained harmonic and instrumental color, hot emotions, and intense poetic tenderness. Audiences—whether in the literary, visual, or musical arts—were not merely to be entertained but transported. Music was considered the superb medium of heightened communication of these values. It went far beyond the limitations of words. "In the mirror of tones the human heart yearns to know itself; it is how we learn to feel feelings," the poet Schiller explained. Feelings were critical. Political views concerning the rights of the individual found their counterparts in the right of an individual artist to "do his thing." For composers, this meant having the right to voice and even to design their own distinctive, personal style. For performers this meant having the right to distinctive, individual, and sometimes flamboyantly eccentric presentations.

Why Did Music Change after Classical "Perfection"?

Music often changes because society changes. As European countries responded to the French Revolution (1789) and other major societal and economic changes, classical style was no longer representative or responsive to one of the new missions of music: to move the heart and soul. The classical era had mirrored the confidence, elegance, and objectivity stimulated by the Enlightenment faith in intellectual power. In that atmosphere music accompanied the life of manners, order, and gentility. Eventually, such rationalism became an inhibitor rather than an inspiration. The "predictability" of the Newtonian world could not embrace or countenance the deep emotions and unpredictability of the human experience. Romantic philosophy led music to a new mission: to reflect human experience and emotions. Music was both a mirror and a passage into the soul of man. Individual experience, especially pathological or neurotic experience, and its expression were prized. In poetry, for example, the subject pronoun "I" became significant. The words of the great romantic poet Shelly are typical of the angst, yearning, and cultivated dilemmas of the romantic spirit:

> Oh, lift me as a wave, a leaf, a cloud!
> I fall upon the thorns of life! I bleed! ("Ode to the West Wind")

The romantic mind was enchanted by the mystery and drama of a world which could not be rationally explained or tamed. Emotions, not rationality, were a valued source of truth. In the words of the great philosopher Kant, music was no less than "the Art of the beautiful play of emotions." Wilhelm Heinse, a novelist of the late eighteenth century, anticipated nineteenth-century thinking when he wrote, "Our feeling is nothing but inner music. . . . Music represents the inner feelings in the exterior air." The romantic world was intoxicated by music's effect. Audiences wanted to be aurally seduced. Musical values, aesthetics, and expectations were reformulated to meet and to match the new thinking and desires.

Beethoven's repertoire exemplifies the stylistic transition from the classical into the romantic world. His early works were clearly derived from and disciplined by Viennese classicism in style and content. Ultimately, his intent, mission, and voice could not be contained in such constraints. Letting go of classical conventions and venturing into personal modes of expression and conviction opened a new world of musical behavior, content, and possibilities. Once "out of the bottle" the romantic genie could never be put back. Beethoven's heart as well as his intellect, his raison d'être, and his soul were embedded and revealed in his music.

His famous letter, called the Heiligenstadt Testament, written when the composer was considering suicide, speaks to his musical commitment in an unforgettable passage: "It seemed impossible to leave the world until I had produced all that I felt called upon to produce and so I endure this wretched existence." He struggled to achieve musical perfection, and extensive notebooks reflect that struggle to communicate via music and to inspire humanity to better spiritual lives. Toward the end of his own life he wrote, "The real artist has no pride. Unfortunately he sees that his art has no limits, and he feels obscurely how far he is from the goal. And while he is perhaps being admired by others, he mourns the fact that he has not yet reached the point to which his better genius, like a distant sun, ever beckons him."

Beethoven's absolute dedication to his art, his elevation of music to a communion with God, and his extraordinary talent bequeathed definitive masterpieces which remain models of perfection and inspiration to all composers who followed. Even Brahms, later in the nineteenth century, wrote, "You will never know how the likes of us feel when we hear the tramp of a giant like Beethoven behind us," according to David Ewen in *The Complete Book of Classical Music*. Truly, Beethoven ushered in and lit the fire for the romantic future.

How to Ignite Music from Classical Restraint to Expressive Romanticism

Instrumental color, melodic lushness, and dynamic extremes were cultivated by the romantic composers to make music more emotional and affecting. Instruments were combined in imaginative ways to create lush composite sounds, thereby replacing the clarity cherished in the classical taste. Soaring, extended melodies swept the listener to thrilling vistas, and intimate melodies quietly confided intimate emotions. Most of the neat boundaries and proportions of classical forms were stretched, adapted, and finally by mid-century discarded to meet the requirements of artistic fulfillment and personal exotic statements within the romantic style.

Changes in Musical Form and Behavior: Growth and Elasticity

As certain classical conventions were replaced there were massive consequences. Abandoning compliance with the classical strictures of sonata-allegro form allowed symphonies to grow to larger sizes as a new logic gained its hold. Romantic composers attained cohesiveness in several new ways. Allowing themes to migrate from movement to movement connected large works, and sometimes a story line dictated the form (as in program music) or emotions and ideas (in tone poems) generated an adhesive which would hold the whole piece together. Internal rather than external forces frequently influenced musical flow and architecture. Symphonic scale expanded, particularly within extended development sections and large codas.

Melodies swelled to larger proportions and were colored by new kinds of chords, increasing the desired emotional impact. As a consequence, the basic Western tonal system was eventually compromised by the new harmonic freedom. Coloristic emphasis weakened functional harmony, and compounding that weakening we find other harmonic behaviors, such as free modulation (moving at will rather than by rule to different keys) and unprepared changes of a tonal center. Such harmonic tampering would have vast consequences in the twentieth century.

Taking a cue from Darwinian evolutionary concepts, music sometimes reflected evolutionary logic in its forms. Organic process rather

FIGURE 2.8. A 423-member orchestra and choir performs Mahler's "Symphony of a Thousand." Photo courtesy of the University of Victoria.

than clearly demarked architectural sections became a compositional logic. At times, entire symphonies emerged in one vast movement, or several movements ran together rather than stopping between separated sections, such as in Schumann's Fourth Symphony. In this work the composer specifically ordered that the movements be played without pause. In place of contrasting themes (one of the essential points of classical sonata-allegro format), he focused on the same theme throughout the work. Concepts such as Liszt's thematic transformation were similarly organic. In this process a single idea was explored in many iterations (evolutions) on a large scale. Unlike the Schumann process in which the theme remained basically unchanged, in the Liszt version of a single theme the theme itself becomes transformed and matured.

Orchestral Changes

The classical orchestra was inadequate to meet the romantic aesthetic. Orchestras grew to enormous proportions. Perhaps the most extensive statement of this was Mahler's Symphony of a Thousand, which included a chorus of 450! Berlioz's *Requiem* required no less than twelve horns and sixteen trombones!

In strings, the popular compositional practice of dividing the parts resulted in enriching and deepening the texture. Across the board, playing in high or low ranges added potential coloration. Violas and lower strings were no longer relegated to "filling in" but were given melodic duties. Vibrato (created by shaking the hand on the fingerboard) added more opportunity to enrich the sound by rapid alternation of the intonation. When you see string players' hands shaking on the fingerboard it is not because they are nervous, but rather because they are deftly altering a single pitch.

Brass players welcomed improvement in the valve system, which lengthened the tubes and provided new notes which would generate additional overtones. More notes were possible. Trombones entered the picture. Writing quietly for brass added an iridescent popular timbre. Timpani were increased in number and tuned to produce various chords. And they became melodic instruments too.

The whole question of choosing which instruments played a part (called orchestration) became very important. Many textbooks on the art of orchestration emerged. One of the most famous was written by Nikolay Rimsky-Korsakov, who felt that orchestration was an essential part of musical composition. The voice in which the music spoke, for Rimsky-Korsakov, was a critical decision.

The Emergence of "Star" Performers

In the midst of all the musical changes special musical showmen entered the scene: the instrumental virtuosos. These were superstar, athletic performers whose abilities to show off their prowess became a hit. Brilliant concerti and solo recitals were their stock-in-trade. Sometimes these musicians (usually pianists and violinists) accompanied their performances with exciting extramusical drama. Paganini swept onto the stage in a black cloak, and it was said he played a violin with strings made from the intestines of a late wife! He was also considered to be in league with the devil in order to play with such wizardry, and some suggested that his feet were really hoofs (see p. 91, fig. 3.12, for an example of Paganini's music).

Franz Liszt's performances were also legendary, as he pranced on stage and threw his white gloves on the floor before playing. His keyboard technique was indeed amazing in and of itself, but he would further dazzle by shaking his head, thereby creating a vast swirl of golden hair that created a halo effect. Women flocked to his concerts and avidly picked up his cigar butts and placed them in their bosoms! Offstage, the virtuosos often led spectacular rule-breaking lives, and the accounts of their marriages, affairs, and children outdo any soap opera. In this case, however, their personal life stories usually have a basis in truth.

The Lifestyle for Composers Changes

The old patronage system was dead. Composers and performers now had to make their way in a commercial world. They had to sell tickets to concerts, require concert fees, and earn their way. Frequently they taught at conservatories or universities to make ends meet. All too often they lived in dire poverty or, like Schubert, were supported by friends who believed in them. In spite of its emotion and beauty, the siren call of music was a hard career choice.

Emotion, Expressiveness, Individuality, and Sensuality

Romantic music was meant to enchant. New linkages to literature and painting increased inspirational music options. Amateur musicians flourished, and music moved into homes as well as concert halls. The piano became a vital transmitter of the romantic sound, and just having a piano in one's home was a sign of cultivated taste. Individualism also manifested itself in the nationalist voices which emerged in the latter part of the century. Music which voiced the inflections of faraway lands and folk music found a place in the romantic taste for the exotic, historic, and colorful.

The nineteenth century was musically vibrant and explosive: the romantic stimulus generated a huge repertoire of enormous beauty and delight which consistently lies close to our hearts. Many of our favorite composers, such as Rachmaninoff, Schumann, Brahms, Wagner, Tchaikovsky, Schubert, Berlioz, Dvořák, Saint-Saëns, Mendelssohn, and Liszt populated those extraordinary years. In the end, the inspiring romantic vitality was consumed by its own overheated passions and intensity. In the work of the very late romantic composers who were writing between 1890 and 1910 (sometimes called post-romantic composers), it became clear that music had reached and perhaps surpassed the summit of romantic style in grandiose proportions. In Mahler's viewpoint, writing a symphony was no less than creating an entire world. His symphonies were gargantuan products, subject to critical acclaim and critical derision. Sometimes his works were called hysterical and bombastic, and at other times his works were considered to be deeply spiritual, extensive journeys into the soul. Regarding his Third Symphony, Mahler explained his intent, saying, "my work forms a musical poem embracing all the steps in cosmic development in regular ascending order," (quoted in David Ewen's *The Complete Book of Classical Music*). His efforts were based on large concepts, which determined the size.

The early twentieth century reacted against such monumental creations, much as the classical had moved away from the grandiose and complicated statements of the late baroque. Yet the potency and innovations of the romantic aesthetic would not be entirely extinguished. Certain parts of the romantic aesthetic eventually were rekindled or referenced in the works of certain major twentieth-century composers. As in most musical eras, the successive time zones overlapped: romanticism and its tenets smoldered as the modern world emerged.

THE ROMANTIC FINGERPRINT

- emotional
- personalized, individual expression most important
- large-scale forms, ensembles, and durations
- linked to other arts, such as painting, literature, and poetry
- virtuosic: stars such as Paganini and Liszt created a new model for performers and composers

Romantic composers (see chapter 4, "Classical Music Sampler," for descriptions): Beethoven (later works), Berlioz, Bizet, Brahms, Dvořák, Elgar, Franck, Grieg, Janáček, Liszt, Mendelssohn, Mussorgsky, Rachmaninoff, Respighi, Rimsky-Korsakov, Rossini, Saint-Saëns, Schubert, Schumann, Sibelius, Johann Strauss Jr., Richard Strauss, Tchaikovsky, Wagner

PLATE 1. Pietro da Cortona, ceiling painting,
Glorification of the Rule of Urban VIII.
Galleria Nazionale d'Arte Antica (Pal. Barberini-Corsini),
Rome, Italy. © Scala/Art Resource, N.Y.

A lavish example of baroque ceiling art: crowded, busy, dramatic,
swirling activity similar to the activity of baroque fugues
and similar polyphonic pieces.

PLATE 2. Peter Paul Rubens,
Minerva Protects Pax from Mars ("Peace and War").
© National Gallery, London, 2003.

Notice the high color contrasts and the contrasts of the
subject matter: peace and war. Baroque art and music savored the idea
of contrasts, especially in juxtaposition.

PLATE 3. Bernini, *The Ecstasy of St. Theresa*. Cornaro Chapel, S. Maria della Vittoria, Rome, Italy. © Scala/ Art Resource, N.Y.

St. Theresa and the angel are brightly illumined by sunlight in a side chapel of the Church of Santa Maria della Vittoria. As in the Rubens, we find the high drama of chiaroscuro. The release of high emotions and drama echo the exuberant emotional thrust and drama of baroque music. The support of the figures is barely noticeable, and this theatrical effect would have also been pleasing in the dramatic statements of baroque music.

PLATE 4. *Louis XIV, the Sun King.* Bibliothèque nationale de France, Paris.

The Sun King's lavish costume of flashing rays reflects the extravagance and imaginative freedoms inhabiting the baroque appetite for dramatic impact.

PLATE 5. Jean-Honoré
Fragonard, *The Swing.*
Reproduced by permission of
the Trustees of the Wallace
Collection, London.

Typical of the rococo period,
this portrait of idyllic innocence
echoes the grace and delicacy
of its musical counterpart.

PLATE 6. Antoine Watteau, *The Embarkation for Cythera.* Charlottenburg Castle,
Staatliche Schloesser und Gaerten, Berlin, Germany. © Scala/Art Resource, N.Y.

An elegant, idyllic scene similar to the graceful *gallant* music of the rococo.
Delicacy and discrete colors are hallmarks of the composition, similar to
the delicacy of rococo themes and harmonic coloration. Used as
inspiration for Debussy's piano piece *L'isle joyeuse.*

PLATE 7. John Martin, *The Great Day of His Wrath*.
© Tate, London, 2002.

A roaring example of romantic fervor. The overwhelming power of untamed
nature is released in all its fury; the drama of a vengeful God and the small
humans helpless in the hands of fate echoes the heated, thunderous music of
the romantic. The helpless position of man (subject to fate or
to inner torments) was a popular theme.

Above: PLATE 8. Camille Corot, *Dance of the Nymphs.*
© Réunion des Musées Nationaux/Art Resource, N.Y.

Another type of romantic landscape: a magical, elegant, sentimental, and thoroughly "benign" scene. A transporting vision similar to romantic pastoral music, which provides enchanting and transporting music. The painting, like romantic music, is strongly emotionally appealing.

Top right: PLATE 9. George Caleb Bingham, *Fur Traders Descending the Missouri.* The Metropolitan Museum of Art, Morris K. Jesup Fund, 1933. (33.61) Photograph © 1992 The Metropolitan Museum of Art.

A sentimental view of nature: gentle light and all is at peace, complete with a soft cat to domesticate the scene. The two fur traders are relaxed and calm in an idyllic, misty setting. The surface prettiness of the painting is similarly reflected in the prettiness of many romantic pieces, especially those known as "miniatures."

Bottom right: PLATE 10. Henry Fuseli, *The Nightmare,* 1781. Founders Society purchase with funds from Mr. and Mrs. Bert L. Smokler and Mr. and Mrs. Lawrence A. Fleischman. Photograph © 1997, The Detroit Institute of Arts.

A fine example of Gothic, horrifying romanticism, such as that found in Berlioz's *Symphonie Fantastique.* The mind has been taken over by demons seeming to emerge from medieval horror stories. The recesses of the mind are as frightening as anywhere on earth. The psychological dramas within certain nineteenth-century repertoire can be exemplified in the picture.

Above: PLATE 11. Théodore Rousseau, *The Forest of Fontainebleau, Morning*.
Reproduced by permission of the Trustees of the Wallace Collection, London.

A sweetened view of a pastoral scene, idealizing the countryside.
Romantic music similarly idealized the countryside, and folkloric
elements were often quoted in romantic music.

Top right: PLATE 12. Eugène Delacroix, *Death of Sardanapalus*.
© Réunion des Musées Nationaux/Art Resource, N.Y.

High-intensity emotion and color abound in this painting.
The exotic topic (inspired by Lord Byron's drama of 1821) and its
presentation share a kinship with romantic music, which also savored
high emotional intensity, the exotic magnetism of faraway lands
(in this case, Greece), and vibrant color.

Bottom right: PLATE 13. Paul Signac, *Papal Palace at Avignon*.
© 2002 Artists Rights Society (ARS), New York/ADAGP, Paris.
Photograph © Scala/Art Resource, N.Y.

A marvelous example of impressionist style in the shimmering
lighting, the delicate colorations, and the momentary nature of the
light. Impressionist music shimmers and is orchestrated in iridescent
hues, and, as in this painting, such colors (whether of tones or paint)
blend by juxtaposition.

PLATE 14. Edgar Degas, *The Star (or) Dancer on the Stage.*
© Erich Lessing/Art Resource, N.Y.

A classic example of impressionist painting which plays on the
effect of stage lighting on the dancer's skin and costume.

PLATE 15. Claude Monet, *La Gare Saint Lazare.*
© Erich Lessing/Art Resource, N.Y.

Another fine example of impressionist style: suggestive, sensual, an intention to
create only an impression, with subtle coloration and deliberately blurred outlines.
In impressionist music, melodies were sometimes blurred in their outlines, often
their shape and movement were sensual and free, leaving only—as does
the painting—the impression of a fleeting special moment.

PLATE 16. René Magritte, *This is not a Pipe.*
© 2002 C. Herscovici, Brussels/Artists Rights Society (ARS), N.Y.

An "in your face" challenge to rethink standard perceptions and ideas, especially about "what is real." Modern music in its iconoclastic, sometimes sassy manner makes you think and reconsider the nature of "what you know about music" and "what it is" as well.

PLATE 17. Jackson Pollock, *Full Fathom Five.*
© 2002 The Pollock-Krasner Foundation/Artists Rights Society (ARS), N.Y.
The Museum of Modern Art/SCALA/Art Resource, N.Y.

A painting which is created by dripping paint, smearing paint, and throwing paint with knives, buckets, and sticks onto a canvas. Similar to aleatoric music, which is also created by chance; the end result, like this painting, is an outcome that attempts to remove some level of control and intent from the composer.

Above: PLATE 18. Salvador Dalí, *Apparition of Face and Fruit-Bowl on a Beach*.
© 2002 Salvador Dalí, Gala-Salvador Dalí Foundation/Artists Rights Society (ARS),
N.Y. Wadsworth Atheneum, Hartford, Conn. The Ella Gallup Sumner and
Mary Catlin Sumner Collection Fund.

An inquiry into the far edges of art and mixing of dream and reality—an excursion
into the unknown. Akin to musical avant-garde inquiries into the nature of sound
and music, this painting results in startling and sometimes scary answers.

Top right: PLATE 19. Jasper Johns, *Three Flags*.
© Jasper Johns/licensed by VAGA, New York, N.Y. Whitney Museum of American Art,
New York; 50th Anniversary Gift of the Gilman Foundation, Inc., The Lauder
Foundation, A. Alfred Taubman, an anonymous donor, and purchase 80.32.

Jasper Johns is one of the preeminent figures in American pop art. In this work he
takes a recognizable symbol and triples its impact using an ancient medium (encaustic)
which was used by the Greeks for a weighted textured surface. Johns manipulates and
amplifies an everyday image for an artistic statement.

Bottom right: PLATE 20. Charles Sheeler, *Rolling Power*.
Smith College Museum of Art, Northampton, Mass. Purchased, Drayton Hillyer
Fund, 1940.

Like the *sounds* of everyday life in *musique concrète, visions* of everyday life such as
machinery and parts therein became candidates for artistic consideration in the
increasingly industrialized twentieth century.

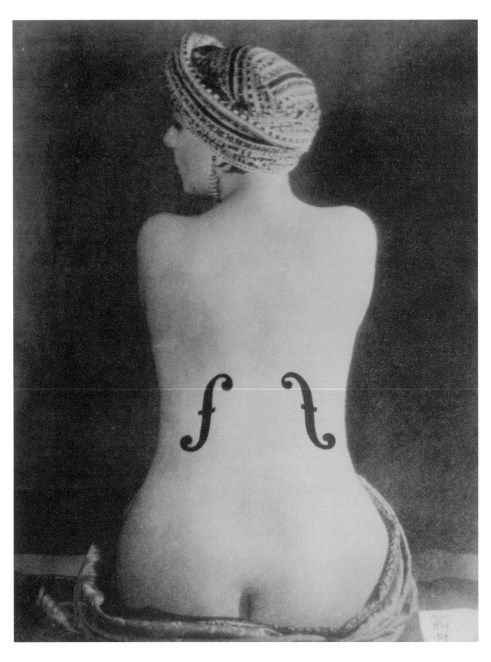

PLATE 21. Man Ray, *Violin of Ingres.*
© 2002 Man Ray Trust/Artists Rights Society (ARS), N.Y.

A vintage twentieth-century blend of music and art.

Suave Impressionism, 1890–1925

It is much to be desired that [Debussy] beware of this
vague impressionism which is one of the most
dangerous enemies of artistic truth.

—Paris conservatory judges assessing
Debussy's cantata *The Blessed Damozel*

As musical romanticism rolled into the later nineteenth century it became inevitable that the wheels would come off. Forecasting this derailment, Claude Debussy, the icon of impressionist music, observed that Richard Wagner, the great German icon of romantic music, was not a prophet. Wagner's *Music of the Future* and music dramas were summations, not roads to the future. Instead, Debussy concluded that Wagner should be placed on the *downward* slope of history. "Wagner," Debussy assessed, "was a sunset, not a dawn."

By the late nineteenth century, romantic music had steadily grown in weight, intensity, complexity, proportion, and subjectivity. In the end, it had attained and exceeded its initial artistic goals. For example, employing hundreds of musicians, and using elaborate stage sets and complex story lines, Wagner's music dramas took hours or even days to perform, as is the case of the four-opera cycle *Ring of the Nibelungen* (1848–52). An unusual late-nineteenth-century composer, Alexander Scriabin, ratcheted romantic inspiration to an even higher notch. For years Scriabin seriously contemplated a multimedia work called *The Mysterium* in which one would find a large orchestra, a chorus, dancers, an olfactory and a color keyboard, poetry readings, and bells: all suspended from zeppelins. To experience all of this required extensive travel because *The Mysterium* was to be held in a special amphitheater in India!

As quoted earlier, Gustav Mahler considered writing a symphony to be no less than "creating a world." By the late nineteenth and early twentieth century, the sheer bulk, extravagance, high dynamic temperatures, and mission of music as a transporter brought romanticism to a blistering conclusion.

Musical impressionism offered a cool, refreshing alternative to all that heat and intensity. As the name implies, impressionism was meant "to give an impression." The concept was birthed and nourished in

France where, since the mid-1870s, composers had started to react negatively to "romantic excesses," especially those of German composers. The French composer Eric Satie noted, "I explained to Debussy how we French needed to break away from the Wagnerian adventure. . . . And, I told him that we needed music of our own, preferably without sauerkraut." Directional cues derived from two extramusical sources:

- impressionist painters, such as Pissarro, Monet, Degas, Manet, and Renoir; and
- symbolist poets, such as Verlaine, Mallarmé, and Baudelaire.

In their dreamy canvases, impressionist painters blurred outlines and allowed colors to melt into one another (see plates 13 and 14). Short brushstrokes replaced long, extravagant lines, permitting a visual experience in which the colors magically blended. Charmed by the transient effects of light and color in nature, these artists found suitable subjects in landscapes, seascapes, and the lives of everyday people. Sunsets, fog, moonlight, water, and fireworks shimmer on their canvases. Inspiration came from without, not from within oneself. Visual stimuli were important, especially changing images (such as water, sunlight, fog, etc.), which were fertile inspiration for musical thought.

Symbolist poets also sought to create an impression and to evoke a poetic image. Verlaine explained, "We desire above all nuance, Not color but half shades. Nuance alone unites dream with dream." These poets used words to stimulate and to suggest an image and to act as symbol. Hence, the name *symbolist*.

At times, visual and literary impressionism combined beautifully with the new music. Debussy's famous work *Prelude to "The Afternoon of a Faun"* was based on a poem by Mallarmé. In his songs, Debussy often used the words of symbolist poets, such as Verlaine. Such relationships between music and the word in impressionism were polar opposites from the complexity of "tone language" and word language systems developed in the nineteenth century.

When disconnected from its poetic inspiration, impressionist music intended to project a beautiful moment or a sensory effect. It was not concerned with broadcasting an overwhelming experience in a gran-

FIGURE 2.9. Marcel Baschet, portrait of Claude Debussy in Rome in 1884. © Giraudon/ Art Resource, N.Y.

diose setting. Nor was it involved with educating and transforming the audience to a higher plane of existence. With atmospheric goals in mind, it was inevitable that the basic elements of music, cloaked in heavy romantic attire, would not do. Harmony, melody, and rhythm were transformed to meet the impressionist mission.

Accompanying these transformations, form and tonality were inevitably affected as well. Many critics, particularly in the early days, found such transformations to be no less than traitorous. "This vague impressionism is one of the most dangerous enemies to artistic truth," the venerable Paris Conservatoire trumpeted. Emilie Cardon, a contemporary art critic, wrote, "the debaucheries of this (impressionist) school are nauseating." Claude Debussy had a revealing conversation with his composition teacher which encapsulates the situation: after playing an impressionist-style piece he had written, Debussy asked his teacher, "Do you find this lovely?" The teacher, Monsieur Guiraud, responded savagely, "This is theoretically absurd!" Debussy explained, "There is no theory! You merely have to listen. *Pleasure and effect* is the law."

Monsieur Guiraud, like many others, correctly sensed danger to the status quo.

Indeed, it was Debussy who launched and defined musical impressionism in his orchestral *Prelude to "The Afternoon of a Faun,"* three nocturnes for orchestra, three symphonic sketches of *The Sea,* and numerous small piano works. The orchestral works featured harp glissandi, wordless choruses, whole tone scales, and other "exotic" effects (see pp. 132–133 for more on *The Sea*).

Where Did the Name Come From?

The term *impressionism* derived from a painting by Claude Monet in 1872–73 titled *Impression: Soleil levante* (Impression: Sunrise). At first the term was derogatory, but gradually it shed pejorative connotations, and artists themselves embraced the identity with enthusiasm. The impressionist aesthetic eventually included poets, painters, and musicians, not only in France but throughout Europe and America.

The Suave Revolution

In its quiet way, musical impressionism was revolutionary. Perhaps never has a revolution been so well mannered and persuasive. In place of boiling dramatic impulses, impressionist composers spoke in relaxed, almost understated terms. Climaxes were more like gentle swells or sumptuous exuberance rather than fiery, sulfurous explosions.

Impressionism did not dissolve all traces of romanticism, and there are some who would argue that it was indeed a logical outcome of romanticism itself. Indeed, the baby was not thrown out with the bathwater. Elements of romantic taste survived but were refashioned in behavior and structure.

For example, the romantic love of harmonic color persisted but was refocused. The chromaticism of late-nineteenth-century style found a new home in fascinating chords built by impressionist composers who experimented with composite sounds (made by tacking on distant overtones to chords). Often these pioneering composers even altered the size of the basic chordal building blocks from thirds to fourths (see *interval* in the glossary). Chords were allowed to wander at will rather than be directed by harmonic laws and traditional behavior. Harmony now had a new mission: to create momentary color and then disappear while the music moved unperturbed to another lush sound. Dissonances were often unresolved and allowed simply to hang freely in the air. Distant overtones were cultured to produce new resonances. Debussy insisted that these chords were not radically new, but the context and treatment of the chords, as they emerged and submerged, generated the innovative behavior.

With impressionism, music gained new flexibility, coloration, and freedom in the context of impressionist treatment. In the hands of impressionist composers such as Debussy, Delius, Ravel, Respighi, and Griffes, it also attained a uniquely seductive, glamorous, and beguiling personality. The result was a wonderful treasure-house of new repertoire for orchestras, solo instruments, and chamber ensembles.

Eventually, evanescence, subtlety, sensation, and refinement were limiting and insufficient for long-term development. Many impressionist innovations provided a significant springboard to music of a totally new nature, which would influence and inspire twentieth-century composers.

THE IMPRESSIONIST FINGERPRINT: COLOR, SENSUALITY, AND EXOTICISM

- Melodies moved serenely, often in a meandering style, without the dictates of strong rhythmic contours or the need to drive to a thunderous climax.
- Harmony (supporting chords under the melodies) broke the rules by moving in the heretofore forbidden parallel motion, which created a drifting quality. These chords glowed in the air, offering color but not direction. Sonority for its own sake was sufficient.
- Rhythms became flexible and were not corseted into precise patterns.
- Musical forms were shortened (you do not find big impressionist symphonies, for example) and became more elastic. Development as an intellectual, musical process was basically dropped.
- Titles were used frequently. These titles offered clues for the musical intent, which was to evoke a sensation or image. Sometimes the composer's vision was imaginary, such as Debussy's *Sunken Cathedral*. Sometimes the titles referred to everyday images, as with pieces such as

Clouds or The Sea. Sometimes the titles referred to sensual experiences, as with *Perfumes Turning in the Air*. Titles for impressionists did not have narrative connotations in the sense of telling a story.
- Special scales competed with the familiar major-minor tonal system. Sometimes these scales came from ancient scales used by the Greeks, from the Far East, or were whole tone scales (scales in which all tones are separated by whole steps).
- Emotion became cool, almost depersonalized.
- Orchestration created exotic, sensuous sounds using new and unexpected combinations of instruments. Often, it would emphasize the "cool" sound of woodwinds over the strings favored by romantics.

Impressionist composers (see chapter 4, "Classical Music Sampler," for descriptions): Debussy, De Falla, Ravel

The Fragmented Twentieth Century

The [avant-garde] of modernism imprisoned music in the academy where it was jealously professionalized, isolated, and rendered sterile, its vital covenant with the general public arrogantly broken.

—Ian McEwan, *Amsterdam*

Unlike previous centuries, which revealed a basic consistency of style, the pendulum of musical life in the twentieth century would swing in many independent directions. Eric Salzman, an astute chronicler of twentieth-century music, summarized, "The development of creative musical thought since 1900 has been rich and complex, full of remarkable achievements, remarkable and unremarkable failures, enormous and continuing promise, and seemingly endless contradiction." However, the twentieth century is much more than wild experimentation, and as the century progressed things calmed down. For Western music, these hundred years were complicated, turbulent, and exhilarating times—in retrospect, like no other.

On one side there was music which offered highly controlled statements; on another side there was music which was totally free in expression. Traditional instruments were used, but they were sometimes played with completely new techniques. Their voices became quite different. New instruments for music making entered the scene. Why did this happen? Our modern times, in spite of all the novelty, were simply addressing an old question first raised in the Middle Ages: "Musica est?" (Music is?). In a quest to be modern in a modern age, this question was answered in striking and sometimes shocking responses.

Some of the answers to "Musica est?" and schools of "music" in the twentieth century were the following:

1. There were novel, experimental schools in which musical constructions, sounds, and forms diverged radically from all that had come before. Jettisoning the past became a cool, clever, modern stance. Predictably, a lot of this music left general audiences in a state of confusion and produced a listening attitude of grim endurance. The new musical "language" was not only foreign, but also seemed driven by mysterious and incomprehensible forces understood and appreciated only by "those in the know." As the twentieth century turned, Arnold Schoenberg's explorations into the nature of atonality created a new musical language. In that language, tones became independent from their tonal relationship to one another. Tonality weakened by the chromaticism of the late nineteenth century, succumbed to a new adventure in sound in which the tones were all "equal" rather than structured in a hierarchy of relationships within a tonal scale or key. The result was musical pieces which were "strange," difficult to follow, and totally unconnected to the past. For many listeners, atonal music seemed more engineered than composed; even worse, the composers seemed to be conversing amongst themselves rather than communicating anything to their audiences.
2. As the century progressed, some musical voices echoed the past in neobaroque, neoclassical, and neoromantic inflections by revisiting the old concept of tonality and the viability of old forms. In this repertoire, both composers and general audiences found familiar and surprisingly fertile territory.
3. Trends which incorporated non-European musical cultures, importing elements of their music and instruments into Western

musical statements. Such inclusion colored, informed, and enriched Western musical expression.

4. The modern age birthed electronic and computer-generated music, digitally recording sound stored in binary numbers, offering a sonic palette which was totally unrelated to anything that had gone before. Electroacoustic music opened a totally new field of musical inquiry. Magnetic tape and computers offered composers the option to write without requiring human musicians at their disposal. Electronic generators and electronic instruments such as synthesizers sometimes joined forces with traditional instruments and sometimes stood on their own for twentieth-century music making. We even find music made by algorithms, performances by musical robots (some controlled by more than sixty computers), and compositions wherein composers, technicians, and computers interacted. Now the possibility of quarter-tones and even smaller intervals were possible, and microtonal music emerged from the new sources.

5. America marched onto the world stage to its own drummer with many gifted composers. Aaron Copland, Charles Ives, Leonard Bernstein, and Samuel Barber (to name only a few) convincingly projected and created "the American sound" both in choral and instrumental settings. Elements of jazz, popular tunes, and folk music often crossed over into "serious" music, lending an unmistakable American personality and inflection.

As composers responded to the eclectic nature of these times, they looked forward, inward, and backward to non-European sources and electronic media for expression. In so doing, they generated a vast repertoire of distinctive, compelling music. Debussy once commented, "An age which makes airplanes should have its own music." Indeed it did.

Debussy also prophetically commented, "Any sounds in any combination and in any succession are henceforth free to be used in a musical continuity." With such unbridled freedom, composers were, more than ever before, unleashed.

Predictably, an unfortunate alienation, bordering on hostility, between audience and serious composer occurred. People wondered, were these composers messiahs or antichrists? Were they charlatans or valid composers? Compounding the situation, the new radical musical experimenters were often unconcerned with "accessibility." When asked if the public was necessary at all, the twentieth-century composer Lukas Foss responded, "the public as such, no. Other people in the same boat, yes." Milton Babbitt echoed that sentiment, commenting that there were two groups of composers: the "academic" (wherein he placed himself) and the "theatrical" (those who wrote for audiences, whom he further described as the "show-biz crowd"). Such attitudes might well explain the relatively small audiences who "appreciated" or even "understood" what in the world was going on in some twentieth-century explorations. General audiences who innocently went to concerts of twentieth-century music felt lost and wondered legitimately, "Where is the music" and "Can I have my money back?"

Looking Forward: Experimental Music

An important twentieth-century French composer, Edgar Varèse, justified experimental music statements, saying, "The experimenting has been done. It is up to the listener to experiment. There is no such thing as avant-garde. There are only people who are a little late." For many audiences, whether late or not, much of the new music was startling, confusing, and not "listener friendly." Yet if the experimental musical outcomes were sometimes "bizarre," the basic questions being addressed were not. Questions and inquiry into such topics as the role of silence in music, organization in musical structure, and the nature of musical material itself had legitimacy. It was some of the answers and responses to the new musical frontiers which created shock.

The Emancipation of Rhythm: Rhythm Moves into the Spotlight

One of the early musical bombshells of the twentieth century was Igor Stravinsky's *Le sacre du printemps* (*The Rite of Spring*). If you want to hear one of the first major breaks with the past, this is the piece (see fig. 3.21 for an excerpt). "Barbaric rhythms" shudder throughout the score; tumultuous orchestral writing adds to the fray. Repetitious statements of themes were hypnotic. Many have connected such "neo-primitivism" with the Parisian artists of the Fauve. "Very little tradition lies behind *Le Sacre* and no theory. I had only my ear to help me. . . . I am the vessel through which *Le Sacre* passed," Stravinsky commented in 1955. His iconoclastic work premiered in Paris in 1913, and the event was greeted with well-documented catcalls, screams, physical fights, spitting, and tomato throwing. The audience was furious, sometimes stamping their feet so hard one could barely hear the music. Although some attendees such as Ravel and Debussy pronounced the work the product of a genius, they were the minority. As the piece traveled on to England in June of 1913, a prominent critic remarked, "A crowd of savages might have produced such noises." In America, the Boston premier eleven years later in 1924 still raised a wild fury. But as musical exploration continued, this piece became more of a friend than a fiend. It was mild in comparison to what was yet to come.

Almost single-handedly, Stravinsky had "emancipated" the role of rhythm in a musical piece, and in this emancipation a new repertoire was unleashed. Edgar Varèse's *Ionisation,* written for percussion alone, is a classic. Other composers, fascinated by a purely percussive palette, produced works such as *Double Music* (John Cage and Lou Harrison) and *Pulse* (Henry Cowell). Occasionally strings were joined with percussion, but usually sparingly because of their expressive quality, such as in *The Two and the One* (Harvey Sollberger).

Exotic rhythms coming from the East began to find a musical presence in the West. Hindu rhythms appeared in Olivier Messiaen's *L'ascension,* and Balinese gamelan rhythmic formulae in *Turangalila-symphonie* were novel and catchy. "Let us not forget," Messiaen insisted, "that the first, the essential element in music, is rhythm."

Works featuring percussion alone (basically omitting melody) relied on the flexibility and drama of rhythm to propel themselves and maintain interest. Combining several rhythms simultaneously had been a familiar compositional element before the twentieth century, and in fact had appeared in the Renaissance. But twentieth-century composers went beyond the mere mixing of patterns within a constant meter or observing the confines of a bar line. Certain radical combinations of rhythmic and metric patterns sounding simultaneously created situations in which bar lines sometimes did not even coincide on the musical score. Quickly changing meters (time signa-

FIGURE 2.10. Sol LeWitt, *Open Geometric Structure IV.* © 2002 Sol LeWitt/
Artists Rights Society (ARS), N.Y. Courtesy of the Lisson Gallery.
Mathematical rules and a set pattern obviously command the ordering of this
painting. The repetitive pattern is similar to the repetitive row of serialism.

tures) sometimes contributed to a sense of rhythmic stability, and the
music seemed to have a chaotic heartbeat. Messiaen and Luciano Berio
offered exciting works in this field. Metric modulation, championed by
Elliot Carter, was an effort to stabilize the seeming chaos. Assigning a
single note the task of remaining "constant," though moving into many
combinations, provided a unit which was invariable. In this, at least,
something remained secure and stable.

New Times in Old Vienna: Serialism

Vienna, musical home of the great classical period, spawned important musical experimenters in the twentieth century. Arnold Schoenberg and his students Alban Berg and Anton Webern devised a radical
new means for writing music called *serialism.* The control within this
system was the polar opposite of aleatory music.

Serialism was a compositional process based on rationality and the
dictates of a prearranged pattern. It worked independently from the
formulae of the familiar tonal system. In serialism, the composer
created a row (a set of twelve unrepeated tones in an invariable pattern), which determined the course of the notes. For our purposes, the

row can be likened to a "theme." Sometimes the row was presented horizontally, sometimes it was sounded vertically, and sometimes it was run backward and forward at the same time. The overriding rule was that the row had to be sounded in its exact, initial formation and order. The result was music which was exceptionally difficult to follow by the uninitiated and, in some respects, looked better on the page than it sounded in its articulation.

Serialism was an intellectual, objective, complicated, and calculated approach to composition. Eventually, serialism was extended to controlling dynamic levels, articulation, and rhythms, which also became "serialized." The American composer Milton Babbitt extended the control of serialism beyond the row in the 1940s and '50s. His *Composition for Four Instruments* and *Composition for Twelve Instruments* are examples of the extended notion of serialism. Obviously, the system had become increasingly complex as more and more elements were serialized, and "total serialization" had a moment in the sun. For the general audience this serialized music was difficult to follow, appreciate, and enjoy: its sound was not "listener friendly." Iannis Xenakis in "The Crisis of Serial Music" explained that "Linear polyphony destroys itself by its very complexity. What one hears in reality is nothing but a mass of notes in various registers." But for those who want make the effort to study the mechanics and logic behind the sound, serialism offers a fascinating puzzle and process.

Questing for New Musical Sounds:
Musique Concrète and Electronic Music

Imagine going to a concert where "music" is made with brake drums, hammers, electronic screeches, and cricket clappers. Or perhaps where electric doorbells, exotic gongs (kajars, kemongs, and other non-Western instruments), and a whirling airplane propeller are invoked. John Cage's *Imaginary Landscapes no. 4,* for twelve radios tuned to different stations, is a famous example of aleatory music using "everyday sounds." One of the questions raised was, why can't the sounds of everyday life be candidates for musical thought? *Musique concrète* used sounds from the everyday world as elements of musical expression. Relating to these ideas, Edgar Varèse explained that his intent, and perhaps that of others, was nothing less than "the liberation of sound." He stated, "I refuse to submit myself only to sounds that have already been heard . . . musicians should take up this question in deep earnest with the help of machinery specialists." A new musical aesthetic was gestating.

One of the more interesting applications of musique concrète is in the mixing of these sounds from the everyday world with "regular instruments" and electronic instruments. Now these combinations are commonplace as background "noise" in film scores and commercials, although serious composers such as Mario Davidovsky continue to write musique concrète for the concert hall as well.

Electronic music (music created by electronic means) has been generated by analog and digital synthesizers, computers, oscillators, digital synthesis, workstations, MIDI controllers, tape recorders, microprocessors (at the turn of the twenty-first century), samplers, sequencers, amplified instruments, and pipeless electronic organs. These were mainstream sources for new sounds. Special instruments such as the Doomsday Machine, a miniature synthesizer built inside a saxophone, and the Electar were among many electronic offshoots from mainstream "instruments." Other sources for electronic sounds came from musique concrète ideas wherein, with electronic manipulation, everyday sounds could be re-created (by pitch alteration, reversing, filtering, cutting and splicing, speeding up, slowing down, and mixing) into totally new sources for musical sound.

Electronically generated tones and controls (through computer microchips and programs, light sensitive "instruments," and miniaturized circuitry) opened significant new vistas for musical thought. They produced a new breed of performers (Björk, Eno, and the Pet Shop Boys, for example) and supplied a breed of composers with some new electronic skills or at least good technicians. Splicing and cutting of tape, for example, was an "art." Digital synthesizers and samplers, arriving in the 1970s, made mixing, sound-on-sound, splicing, and so forth much easier, replacing tape splicing and cutting altogether. A curious sound emanating from intentional "miswiring" echoed the old practice of scordatura, an intentional "mistuning" of conventional instruments.

Outside of composers' studios and special concerts, Hollywood provided an early market for the new, somewhat eerie sounds, which were considered desirable for scores of science fiction and horror films, such as *Forbidden Planet*. Rock bands such as the Silver Apples and Pink Floyd produced electronic music almost exclusively. Both in popular and serious formats, with the advent of electronic sources Western music became involved with radically new acoustic adventures.

Music and Technology: A New Marriage

Electronic music created a new relationship between music and technology, both in sound and in compositional practices. Tape and computers generated sounds which offered a totally new world of almost unlimited sound resources. Even well-established twentieth-century composers such as Paul Hindemith and Ernst Toch flirted with the new vistas opened by electronic means. Synthesizers provided new pitches, dynamics, and timbres. Composers in this field now had to be concerned, or at least familiar with, voltage control, amplitude modulation, multitrack recorders, and oscillators! One of the famous pieces in this area was John Cage's *Rozart Mix* (1965), which was played by eighty-eight tape loops emerging from thirteen tape recorders. Milton Babbitt's *Ensembles for Synthesizer* (1961–63) and Karlheinz Stockhausen's *Gesang der Junglinge* (1955–56) created tape-based musical pieces. For all of this, Pierre Boulez noted, "you must have composer and technician alike." Music "technicians" arrived on the scene from places such as Bell Labs, and computer programmers frequently joined with composers to provide software for the new music. Sound designer software by Digidesign, Incorporated, became one of the favorite programs.

So where was the human touch? "A computer is, ideally, perfectly dumb," Paul Lansky commented. "Software is an attempt to give it some intelligence and that intelligence is always going to be a translation of human intelligence of one sort or another." MIDI (musical instrument digital interface) arrived on the scene to connect synthesizers and digital audiotape (DAT), which had become sources of musical creativity. MIT's Media Laboratory devised a program which would hopefully insert the human touch. As David Cope explained in *New Directions in Music,* designers "hard-wired neural-net-learned accompaniments to follow nuances of tempo indicated by human performers connected to the net via contact microphones attached to their instruments." Yet, the human touch in sculpting sound was critically missing in the outcome. Milton Babbitt had a stunning opinion on that problem as well, saying, "the university turns with delight to the electronic field because it is self-contained, requiring neither performance nor publication. The medium provides a kind of full satisfaction for the composer . . . I can send it anywhere in the world knowing exactly how it will sound. . . . I feel closer to members of my Philosophy department than to many who regard themselves as musicians." Clearly, emotional, human communication was not an issue or a goal for him or for many others.

Math, Music, and Tones

Sometimes tones were manipulated and created mechanically, or the traditional "distance" between two adjacent notes became fractured into smaller bits. In this regard, "microtones" emerged on the scene. Some interesting instructions in this regard came from Mario Davidovsky (when he was associate director of the Columbia-Princeton Electronic Music Center), who noted the following while creating a single tone: "I am about to trigger these two envelopes. One sharp attack and short decay using a high band of white noise very loudly will combine with one short attack and a very long decay on a high 3,000 cycle per second sine wave."

Music and technology had made a very unique alliance: for example, math and music. The heart of this idea is that "Any mathematical formula can be translated into an algorithm capable of producing music," according to David Cope's *New Directions in Music.* In this field, computers generally were the "instruments." Machines generated the music (via complex programming systems), which was then transposed to traditional music notation. A DATATRON computer "wrote" *Push Button Bertha,* often considered to be the first completely machine-composed music. How did it do it? In this relatively simple case, David Cope explains, "The operator inspires DATATRON by first keying in a 10 digit random number. This causes the machine to generate and store 1000 single digits, each representing one of the eight diatonic notes in the scale. . . . The program then motivates DATATRON to pick notes at random, testing each for melodic acceptability as it goes along." Pierre Barbaud countered the "inhumanity" of such music by saying, "Algorithmic music is human inasmuch as it is the product of rational beings."

Algorithmic music built up a large following. Even Bell Labs got into the act with the work of James Tenney in his *Four Stochastic Studies* and *Dialogue*. Analysis of existing music was usually the starting point. Moving from this base, programmers took over, creating extensive systems (usually written in BASIC computer language) to generate melodies, chord progressions, and ornaments. They also used "musical signatures," or higher-level syntheses that analyze and reproduce certain motifs and combinations used by composers to replicate their sound. The result was a new composition that sounded like Beethoven's or Mozart's!

MIT's Media Laboratory created "neural nets," which isolated and applied nuances of rhythm, dynamics, and so forth found in human performance and were sometimes invoked to make it all "more musical." Lejaren Hiller's three pieces *Algorithms I, II,* and *III* employed stochastic and random elements, and he was quite proud of the outcome, noting, "Nowadays I think that my computer pieces possess more expressive content than I would have first guessed. I suppose that my programming contains biases that are subjective." Sometimes the beginning point was the *Musikalisches Wurfelspiel* (musical dice games), which were truly "made" for a mathematical-computer approach. But other algorithmic composing instruments also emerged, such as Joe Jones's percussion machine.

Probability theory emerged in Iannis Xenakis's work, and his process uses "vectoral analysis, probability laws, stochastics, Markovian chains, game theory, group theory, set theory Boolean algebra, and Gaussian distributions as formalizations," as David Cope notes. The composer commented that "One must know these mathematical laws which, in any case, are no more than a tight and concise expression of chains of logical reasoning." Xenakis's book *Formalized Music: Thought and Mathematics in Music* is an excellent source for an introduction to the idea. Quoting from Xenakis's book, "It takes time to go from one point to another in space. Can one repeat a phenomenon?" Music when performed by a human differs from performance to performance. "What is time for the musician?" Xenakis inquired. "Music participates both in space outside time and in the temporal

FIGURE 2.11. Frank Gehry, Guggenheim Museum, Bilbao, 1997. © Howard Davis/GreatBuildings.com.

flux. . . . A stroke of the bow is a referential event that can define durations of a fraction of a second." In his chapter concerning time, space, and music, he wrote, "Music is everywhere steeped in time: time in the form of an impalpable flux or time in its frozen form, outside time, made possible by memory."

An investigation into the problem of time and personalization emerged in the UPIC system, which involves "a machine dedicated to the interactive composition of musical scores which will allow recording of a performance." A UPIC score is a collection of notes that are called arcs. An arc is a pitch rather than a time curve. Durations can range from six minutes to the total duration of the musical page (one hour maximum). During performance, the musician can switch from one page to another and may control the tempo and play position by moving the mouse. Composers such as Michel Philippot (in *Composition for Double Orchestra*) tried to make "the most complete inventory possible of the set of my gestures, ideas, mannerisms, decision, and choices which were mine when I wrote the music." Then, he would "reduce this set to a succession of decisions, binary if possible.

And finally, to present this scheme in the form of a flow chart, the operation of which could easily be controlled."

The impulse, over and over, seemed to reduce or altogether avoid the human touch, understandable in a world shredded by two world wars, the Holocaust, the atom bomb, and international terrorism.

Xenakis perhaps answered all his inquiries on his very first page of *Formalized Music* when he wrote, "This transmutation of every-day artistic material which transforms products into meta-art *is a secret. The 'possessed' reach it without knowing its mechanism.*" Nonetheless, he insists that "there is a historical parallel between European music and the successive attempts to explain the world by reason." From this premise he entered into the realm of what he called stochastic music, named "in honor of probability theory."

Mathematical logic and acoustical science has produced "music" to be sure. But at the heart of it all, the art of music will most probably remain "a secret," undiscoverable in numbers or science. Music is related to science but not born of it.

FIGURE 2.12.
Anthropomorphic flutist robot. Developed by Atsuo Takanishi at the Advanced Research Institute for Science and Engineering at Waseda University, Japan. An example of the marriage of high technology and music in the twentieth century.

New Performers and the New Orchestra

Not only machines but new performers were also created in the last quarter of the twentieth century. The Tsukuba Musical Robot, appearing in concert at the 1985 International Exposition in Tsukuba, Japan, is controlled by sixty-seven fiber-optically linked computers. It sat at a Yamaha digital organ and scanned the scores with video cameras in its "eyes," while playing music with metal fingers featuring the joints of the human hand. An anthropomorphic Flutist Robot made by Waseda University's Humanoid Robotics Institute (in the Takanishi Laboratory) and a sax-playing robot of the Hosei University Takashima Laboratory sometimes have played together in concert or with humans. On August 24, 2001, in Sukagawa, the Flutist Robot (equipped with special tonguing and trilling capabilities) played with humans at the Future Industrial Hall. The repertoire included the Mozart Flute Quartet and Mendelssohn Duo, played with a professional flutist and musicians.

The human-robot ensemble birthed a significant problem: issues of timing needed to be resolved, especially because humans will naturally, inevitably vary tempi for expression and emotional reasons. This issue of *kansei,* or human attitude, is being worked on currently at Tsukuba University. The purpose of this project is to imitate sensitive recognition such as sense, feeling, emotion, sensitivity, and psychological reaction in the robot's playing. Its goal is to produce a networked robot with sensations and a program to control it. This, like the MIT neural networks, is another example of attempting to humanize the robot.

Loudspeakers, not live musicians, became an important medium of musical transmission. In this case, audiences did not "see" the performance but listened to the music without visualizing musicians producing the sounds. Thus, a radically new musical experience was created for listeners, along with the works themselves. Manipulation of taped and electronically synthesized sounds created a new musical language within the so-called musical experience. If previously the electronic music was "manipulated" (probably by technicians) at the time of performance, we now had live electronic music. Therein, perhaps, lay the desired but evanescent human touch.

Indeterminacy: Aleatory Music (Chance Music)

The role of chance in music, addressed in the twentieth century, was not a totally new concept. In Latin, *alea* means dice. In the eighteenth century, few examples of chance music existed, ordering the measures with a throw of dice. Known as *Musikalisches Wurfelspiel*, these novel experimentations were more stunts than legitimate inquiry. Even the venerable Haydn and Mozart toyed with this idea.

For certain twentieth-century composers, chance had a serious and greatly expanded role in musical expression and form. American composers Ives and Cowell (in the 1930s) ventured into this. One of the most important leaders in this phenomenon was another American composer, John Cage. His works in aleatory music and explanatory essays were extensive and inspiring to other significant composers such as Morton Feldman, Earl Brown, and Christian Wolff. In his own words, Cage explained his mission, saying, "The purpose of all this purposeless music would be achieved if people learned to listen."

Randomness became a trendy compositional tool, a logic which would ironically be a determinant. The application of indeterminacy was not the same in every case, however. At times randomness governed the entire piece, and at times randomness was confined to specific elements.

Imagine going to a concert where the conductor enters with a shotgun, fires a well-aimed shot at manuscript paper, and then allows the holes to indicate notes and plays the piece for you. Or a concert where the composer hands out the score pages in random order to the musicians and the piece is therefore "different" every time. Or a piece in which the continuity of the work is decided by six flips of three coins while referencing the *I-Ching*, an ancient Chinese philosophic and divination manual. Toshi Ichiyanagi offered a unique aleatory piece titled *Piano Piece no. 5*, in which the performer at the keyboard holds down the sustaining pedal and a partner shoots darts at the back of the piano, creating reverberations. In such works, chance could be said to be "in control" and unlimited.

Sometimes the role of chance was curtailed, allowing its role to be specified and limited, for example, only to dynamics or durations. Stockhausen's *Plus-Minus* (1963) allows for dynamic changes determined by chance, within a defined parameter. Cage's Concerto for Piano and Orchestra (1957–58) allowed vast freedoms both for the soloist and orchestra within a score, including the option of simultaneously playing the concerto with other pieces (chosen by chance) that he had written.

Listening indeed would have been a challenge for those attending a concert of Elliot Schwartz's *Elevator Music* (1967). In this case, the listeners boarded elevators and rode up and down in a twelve-story building. On each floor different performers were playing. As the elevator doors opened and closed (according to the whim of the elevator operator), the mobile audience would hear music which was constantly changing according to the floor at hand. Some floors also included total silence, where nobody was playing. Perhaps not surprisingly, this experiment in "the physical spaces of sound" has not been frequently performed.

Randomness resulted in music which was different and surprising in every performance. The concept predictably generated a lot of controversy. To "make sense," music did seem to require a plan of some sort. By the 1970s music that was entirely aleatoric had basically run its course, although composers still incorporate "controlled" sections of chance music into larger pieces.

FIGURE 2.13. The Thai Elephant Orchestra, directed by Richard Lair and David Soldier. An example of the new types of orchestras and performers in the twentieth century.

Silence and Duration

The role of silence and time in music also became a matter to study. John Cage made the issue quite clear in a famous, and perhaps notorious, piece titled *4'33"*. In 1952 David Tudor, the first pianist to present the piece, sat quietly at the keyboard, lifting and lowering the fall board to denote the three movements (each marked "tacet," which means "do not play") as a clock marked the beginning and end of the work. The piece *4'33"* was, as far as the instrumentalist was concerned, soundless! Sound of any nature during the time the clock was running came from the audience. While *4'33"* was usually "performed" at a piano, "the work may be performed by any instrumentalist or combination of instrumentalists and last any length of time," Cage noted in the score.

Experimentation into the nature and duration of sound was a significant part of the new music. A fascinating "piece" regarding the role of time is *Music for Electric Metronomes* (1960) by Toshi Ichiyanagi, which offers a score of numbers joined in different patterns of lines that refer only to the metronome settings.

Look at some of the instructions for Christian Wolff's *Play* concerning durations (I bet you never had music instructions like this!): "Play, make sounds in short bursts . . . allow various spaces between playing (2, 5 seconds indefinite). . . . One, two, three, four or five times play a long sound or complex or sequence of sounds . . . or a player should play at a signal within 2 or 5 seconds of a signal over which he has no control. At some point or throughout use electricity." Temporal instructions based on uncontrolled signals is a major deviation from the traditional regularity of music beats.

Notation in Experimental Music

Conventional music notation underwent radical changes in the experimental music of the twentieth century. Certain composers such as Morton Feldman, Krzysztof Penderecki, and John Cage sometimes required a totally new system of notation and graphic presentation rather than the familiar notes on a staff. Thus, they created their own musical "notes," which were unlike any seen before. Notes became wedges, dots without stems, and curious lines indicating durations. Sometimes charts and graphs replaced traditional music paper in the new scores. Brown's *December 1952 in Folio,* for example, uses an abstract design without any musical notation as its score!

The written language of music itself became subject to experimentation. In some cases, the traditional music staff (the set of five lines on which music is written) also came under scrutiny and change. George Crumb's *Makrokosmos,* vols. 1 and 2, placed notes on a staff, but the staff itself appeared in a circular pattern, similar to the zodiac, rather than in horizontal lines. In Stockhausen's *Gruppen* the staffs appeared in sections all over the page rather than being stacked upon one another as in traditional score writing.

One of the by-products of aleatory (and computer) music was the necessity to "write" music with new symbols. The old staves and notes would not suffice for the new thinking. Often, notes as we are accustomed to seeing them completely disappeared. The challenge to performers both in reading and in producing such music was enormous.

Traditional Instruments:
New Sounds and Playing Techniques

Traditional instruments sometimes were made to sound different by modification. Prepared pianos emerged: nails, metal, rubber, bolts, plastic, and paper were placed on the strings to create a new pianistic voice. Sometimes pianos were even tuned differently so that the overall pitch of every note was radically altered. Following up on this idea, Emerick Spielmann invented a superpiano, using a method which interrupted light on photoelectric cells, thereby altering the piano's pitch in response to current.

Part of the musical experimentation involved new methods of instrumental performance technique. Krzysztof Penderecki's *Threnody for the Victims of Hiroshima* sometimes required the violins to play using the tailpiece of the instrument, or between the bridge and the tailpiece, areas not used in conventional playing. Piano keyboards were sometimes crushed with a whole forearm rather than fingers in clusters. Sometimes piano strings were plucked from within the body of the instrument by hand or were beaten by drumsticks. Rim shots were no longer only for basketball but were a part of percussionists' techniques, along with crushing dishes, tearing paper, beating with their knuckles, and bowing gongs with a string bass bow.

Other works mixed playing methods, such as bowing a vibraphone in *Percussion Quartet* (1983) by Lukas Foss, and created new scales. Harry Partch developed an "adapted viola," attaching a cello fingerboard to the traditional instrument. He also provided a special scale expanded to twenty-nine rather than the usual twelve tones. Some of his later scales expanded to fifty-five tones in certain microtonal experimentation.

Looking Backward . . .

The twentieth century did not remain singularly focused on radical reforms, computers, and mathematical formulae for its music. Distinguished twentieth-century composers also "looked backward," finding traditions, forms, and sounds from the past which would be incorporated into modern music. In some cases, composers who had been "experimental" shifted gears and reverted to conventional instruments and logic, leaving experimentalism and opting for time-honored methodologies. Audiences, for the most part, were relieved to find something familiar and listener friendly. The following styles, referencing the past, were also features of the twentieth-century musical landscape.

Neoclassical style looks back to the classical period. Sergey Prokofiev, in his *Classical Symphony*, and Stravinsky, the enfant terrible of *The Rite of Spring*, in his Symphony in C and Symphony in Three Movements, echoed classical inflections in their tonality, clarity, and formal constructs.

Neobaroque style looks back to the baroque period. The concerto grosso format and driving rhythms of those times were only two facets which appealed to several major twentieth-century composers. Béla Bartók was exemplary in this regard. His *Music for Strings, Percussion and Celesta* presents itself with baroquelike fugal textures, though working with modern directives.

Neoromantic style looks back to the romantic period. Samuel Barber, Aaron Copland, and Roy Harris were composers whose work often echoed romantic sentiment. Copland's lush *Appalachian Spring* and Prokofiev's *Romeo and Juliet* revived romantic passion, orchestration, and melodies.

In works such as these, the wisdom and creativity of the past were rediscovered and celebrated in the modern world.

Minimalism

"Minimalism is a reaction to information overload, to the buzzing, blooming confusion of a complex industrial society with its multiple and contradictory communications systems and messages," Salzman explained. Four of the big names in this field are Steve Reich, Terry

Figure 2.14. I. M. Pei, Bank of China, Hong Kong.
© Howard Davis/GreatBuildings.com.

Riley, LaMonte Young, and Philip Glass. Music in a minimalist style is usually repetitive, rather delicate, slow moving, and shapeless, and thereby almost hypnotic in its effect. The nickname "trance music" has derived from this repetitive aspect.

Lacking the traditional momentum of tension and release, minimalist music moves calmly and deliberately on a limitless canvas. Frederic Rzewski's *Coming Together* (1917) holds its rhythmic pattern for 394 measures! Features of Asian music, especially the ragas (melodies) and talas (rhythmic patterns) of traditional Indian music, were influential in minimalism; in particular, the sitarist Ravi Shankar was very influential to composers who were involved in this field.

Philip Glass is perhaps the most famous minimalist composer and has achieved an unusual amount of fame for a contemporary composer. In 1985 he was selected as *Musical America*'s 1985 Musician of the Year, and he has appeared on *Saturday Night Live* and *Late Night with David Letterman*! He has written for opera, orchestra, theater, film, dance, and chorus, has collaborated with famous poets such as Allen Ginsberg (*Hydrogen Jukebox*), and has recorded prolifically. If you are looking for examples of minimalist sound, the Philip Glass repertoire and the Philip Glass Ensemble are good sources.

Cross-Fertilization in the Twentieth Century

Eventually, minimalist style moved outside "art music" and influenced rock and pop music. This is only one of the interesting connections that occurred between "serious music" and "pop music" in the twentieth century.

Jazz musicians emerged as serious composers and artists in their own right. The crossover between jazz and blues and serious music was a fascinating development. Maurice Ravel included a blues movement in his Violin Sonata. George Gershwin's *Rhapsody in Blue* (1924) and Copland's Piano Concerto (1926) were refreshing examples of jazz inflections, and several of Leonard Bernstein's best-known works are heavily influenced by jazz.

Today, classically trained musicians such as cellist Yo-Yo Ma and violinist Joshua Bell can be found playing both pop and classical music.

Where Will We Go Next in Music?

For most of us, great music at its core reflects humanity and emotions. Music made by machines, crafted or manipulated by numbers, usually misses the human inspirational element of great music. Inevitably, machines and math create musical patterns with an unavoidable sterility and objectivity. Lacking passion, or worse, inserting "contrived passion," strips music of its human nature.

No one can totally foresee what lies ahead for the twenty-first century. As in the twentieth century, we will undoubtedly find yet unimagined and exciting new music. Answers to the ancient question "Musica est?" will be given in many ways. In the end, after all the experimentation and responses to that question, I have no doubt that the quest for beauty, imagination, and artistic craftsmanship communicating to us all will prevail in the truly significant and potent music yet to come. This is precisely the reason for the longevity of the great repertoire of our classical, enduring musical inheritance which lies at the heart of *Classical Music Without Fear*.

THE TWENTIETH-CENTURY FINGERPRINT

- experimentation in rhythm, form, melody, tuning
- technology through electronically generated and altered sounds
- nontraditional systems of control (serialism) or freedom (chance music, improvisation)
- new techniques for playing old instruments, new notation systems, use of silence
- reinventing the past: neoromantic, neoclassical, neobaroque
- world cultures and cross-fertilization with popular and commercial music, as in minimalism

Twentieth-century composers (see chapter 4, "Classical Music Sampler," for descriptions; some composers are also listed under romantic and impressionist fingerprints): Barber, Bartók, Bernstein, Cage, Carter, Copland, Cowell, Crumb, De Falla, Gershwin, Ives, Prokofiev, Rachmaninoff, Ravel, Schoenberg, Shostakovich, Sibelius, Stravinsky

3

READING MUSIC:
READING A BOOK

Reading music is very similar to reading an article or book, which communicates ideas or a narrative through words. As a child you learned to read, and therefore you are a literate person. Literacy also applies to music, although words are not the medium. Notes and symbols indicating pitch, duration, and articulation are the transmitter of musical thought. Musical phrases, themes, and cadences could be analogized to clauses, sentences, and periods. Reading with expression is similar to playing or singing music with expression: there are pauses (like breaths), and excitement is expressed through increasing loudness and rapid pace. Music communicates. Reading music is simply a matter of musical literacy.

Performing music transmits sound written on the score through an instrument which sends the sound to you. Unlike a book or novel which communicates directly to you through words, music always involves an intermediary (unless you are the musician): the performer or the ensemble. The success of musical communication depends on the musicianship, interpretive skills, sensitivity, historical perspective, imagination, and technique of the performer. In an ensemble or orchestra, all players work as a team in presenting a unified or single interpretation, and this is sculpted and determined by the conductor. If there is no conductor (as in chamber music), the musicians must agree on a unified perspective.

Our Western musical language has evolved over hundreds of years. The study of musical notation is a part of every serious musician's course of study. Even if you are not a musician, seeing musical language is a worthy side trip to our concert guide.

Successfully communicating sound through written symbols was a critical development in the history of Western music. Until there was a way to "write music," music was singularly dependent on memory and aural, or performance, tradition. If there were no way to "write music," it is conceivable that we would have no repertoire. The vast legacy of Western music would inevitably have been lost within the time period in which it existed if there were no way to perpetuate music outside of performance.

Notational methods (how music is expressed in writing) have a long and fascinating history; what we see today is a product of evolution. And notation is still evolving. In twentieth-century music we sometimes see notation which eschews the customary for symbols that are totally new!

Standard Notation

The beginning point for text is a blank page. For music, the beginning point is paper which has sets of lines called *staves*. The staff consists of a five-line set which looks like what can be seen in figure 3.1.

FIGURE 3.1. The staff.

Narrowing the number of lines to five was a development which occurred in the Middle Ages. Before this, musical symbols were sometimes written on as many as twenty lines! Next, a clef written at the beginning of the staff indicates a specific pitch, or sound. Most often there are two basic clefs: the treble or G clef and the bass or F clef (see fig. 3.2).

Treble or G   Bass or F

FIGURE 3.2. Treble or G clef and bass or F clef.

There is another important clef which is not seen as often, called the alto or C clef (see fig. 3.3).

FIGURE 3.3. Alto or C clef.

Notice that each clef is identified by a voice type (treble, alto, bass) as well as by a letter name (explained below). The voice type gives you a good idea where the music on that staff falls in relation to the average singing voice: high (treble), medium (alto), and low (bass). The word *clef* derives from the latin *clavis,* which means "key." You might find it convenient to think of a clef as a key that cracks the musical code, translating the notes which follow.

Notes are placed on, above, and below the staff to show their pitch. It is easy to tell if one pitch is higher than another based on its position on the staff: notes closer to the bottom line are lower than those near the top. Notes are named according to a letter (A–G), and that letter represents a specific pitch. The note names will change depending on which clef is used (see fig. 3.4).

Now you can see why the treble clef is called a G clef: its innermost tip rests on the pitch G. The same thing goes for the F and C clefs.

These pitches can be altered by signs that are placed to their left. These signs include a sharp, which raises the pitch; a flat, which lowers the pitch; and a natural sign, which cancels out a sharp or a flat (see fig. 3.5).

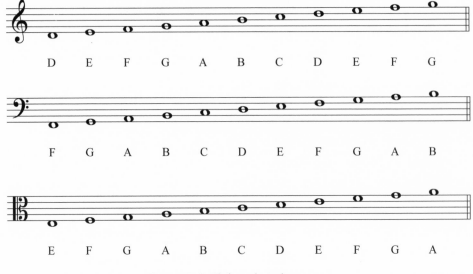

FIGURE 3.4. Clefs and pitch names.

A sharp   A flat   A natural

FIGURE 3.5. Sharp, flat, and natural.

Counting Music: A Very Difficult Matter!

There are two crucial things to keep in mind when counting music:

1. Beats are steady, like heartbeats.
2. Rhythms are patterns imposed over the beat. As you know, music does not hold still. It exists and moves through time. Therefore, indicating time and its divisions is an important part of a musical score.

After the clef there is a set of numbers, one written above the other. This is called the time signature (see fig. 3.6). *It is not a fraction and it does not indicate speed.*

FIGURE 3.6. Time signatures.

The top number indicates the number of beats within the measure (which we will look at, below). The lower number indicates the kind of a note which receives a beat or a fraction of a beat. If the top number is divisible by three (excepting three itself) the number of beats is determined by dividing the top number by three and the bottom number receives a third of a beat. This latter case is called "compound meter."

$\dfrac{3}{4}$ = three beats per measure, a quarter note gets a beat

$\dfrac{2}{4}$ = two beats per measure, a quarter note gets a beat

$\dfrac{4}{4}$ = four beats per measure, a quarter note gets a beat

$\dfrac{9}{8}$ = three beats per measure and a dotted quarter (the sum of three eighth notes) receives a beat

$\dfrac{12}{8}$ = four beats per measure and a dotted quarter (the sum of three eighth notes) receives a beat

Pieces sometimes shift their time signatures. They can do this by designating a different note to receive a beat, or by designating a new number of beats per measure, or both! Alternating meters are indicated by double time signatures at the beginning of the staff.

Simultaneous different meters, or *polyrhythmic meters,* are also used, particularly by modern composers such as Hindemith in *Mathis der Maler* and Stravinsky in *The Rite of Spring.* Ives's Symphony no. 4 is an extreme example of this, in which almost every instrument plays in a different meter (see fig. 3.7). Pieces that use numerous polyrhythmic meters are usually more difficult to perform and rehearse.

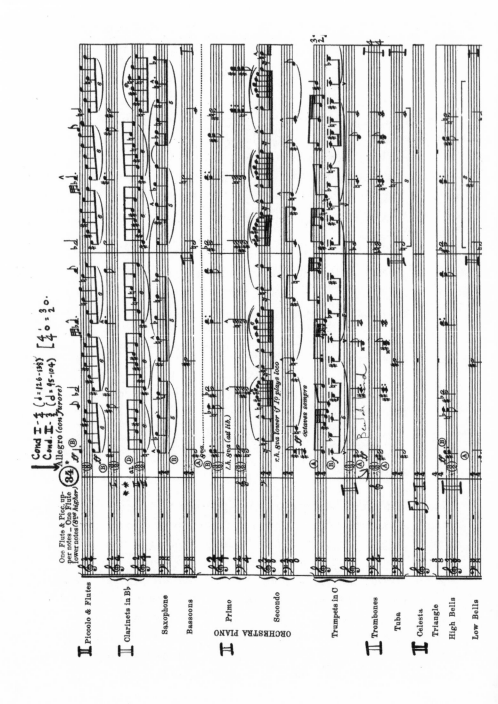

FIGURE 3.7. Charles Ives, Symphony no. 4, second movement. Published by Associated Music-Schirmer. Used by permission. An example of polyrhythmic meters or different time signatures between different parts of the orchestra.

Music can also shift its subdivisions from duple to triple, for example. Thus the beat itself can be cut up into different-sized time components. Irrespective of its components, the beat is invariable unless the composer indicates differently or the performer decides to increase (accelerando) or decrease (ritardando) the speed.

A composer will usually place a word above the top staff at the very beginning, indicating the speed or the mood of the music. From this, the musician will know approximately how fast or slow the music is to be played and with what kind of mood. Usually these words are in Italian, German, or French. For example:

Presto: fast
Presto con fuoco: fast and with fire
Lento: slow
Lento cantabile: slow, with a singing line

In a work with several movements, this label may be used as the movement title. See "A Typical Concert Program Explained" for more (pp. 12–13).

Key Signatures

Often there are other symbols which precede the time signature numbers: sharps and flats. In this case, their number and placement indicate the scale or key being used.

Specifically, a key signature instructs that the indicated note (revealed by line placement of the sharp and flat) is moved a half-step below or above that tone for the duration of the piece. The only exception is indicated by a natural sign within the score itself, which temporarily cancels out the key signature. In figure 3.8, the second B flat is temporarily altered to a B natural.

FIGURE 3.8. Key signature.

Barlines

These vertical lines create segmented, boxlike areas which contain the notes. Each "box," or measure, contains the specific number of beats indicated in the time signature. The notes can be of different durations, but they must add up to the indicated beats in the time signature (see fig. 3.9).

FIGURE 3.9. Bar lines.

Rhythmic Values of Notes

With the staff at the ready, it comes time for the notes. The form of notes has evolved over time as well. At one point, "notes" were in the form of neumes, or little squares. Over time, the neumes took the more familiar round shape we are used to seeing. The straight line is called the *stem*. Stems go up or down and can be on either side of the note, according to placement on the staff. Each note has a different rhythmic value, indicated by its appearance (stem or no stem, note-head filled in or not, etc.).

In figure 3.10, notice how the flags on the stems indicate a doubling of the arabic numeral: these stems are joined together. Paradoxically, as the numbers rise, the time value assigned is cut in half. Two sixteenth notes equal an eighth note, for example. Dots after a note increase its value by one half. In some cases there are doubly dotted notes, which increase the time value again by one half.

FIGURE 3.10. Notes and rhythmic values.

Ornamentation

Ornamentation is exactly what it sounds like: a decoration to the melodic line. Explicit symbols indicate how a note is to be decorated. This involves adding other unwritten notes around the indicated pitch. Ornamentation is a vast topic, subject to many interpretations. One thesis alone weighs in at 604 pages on this issue!

Ornaments are indicated by special symbols which trained musicians read quickly; they then execute the written note in combination with the indicated ornamentation. One of the most common is the trill, in which there is a rapid alternation between the note printed and the upper or lower neighboring tone (see fig. 3.11).

FIGURE 3.11. Trill in notated form and actual sound.

Scores

There are many more symbols for articulation, dynamics, ornamentation, and tempi, which occur within the music. You will see some of these within the score samples which follow. (In music, the word *score* is both a noun and a verb. As a noun, the word refers to the music on the page. As a verb, the word has a broader meaning. To score a piece can mean to set the orchestration, to arrange a transcription, or to produce all the parts in a single presentation.)

Figure 3.12 is a violin score by the star performer and composer Paganini. Notice there is only one staff.

Figure 3.13 is a piano score by Mozart, K. 545. Here there are two staves, one for the right hand and one for the left. There can be three or more staves in more complex works, in which case the right and left hands usually "share" the extra work.

Orchestral scores have shown increasing complexity as more instruments were added to the orchestra. The standard arrangement for an orchestral score is as follows:

THEME

VAR 1

VAR 2

FIGURE 3.12. Paganini, Caprice no. 24 for Violin.

FIGURE 3.13. Mozart, Sonata K. 545 for Piano.

- winds are at the top
- brass is underneath the winds
- percussion is under the brass
- strings are at the bottom (usually four staves for first and second violins, violas, and celli)

Each of these segments is subdivided so that the higher instruments in each group are on top of their section. For example, in the wind section the flute parts are above the bassoons; the violins are higher than the double basses. Notice that the staves for each section of instruments are connected by vertical bar lines, and that the measures are usually numbered for rehearsal convenience.

Individual players see only their parts. A good conductor, however, must master all the parts, read them simultaneously, and direct the orchestra with total fluency and intent to sculpt the work at hand. His or her score has all the parts included on the page, as in the first page of Beethoven's *Coriolan* Overture (see fig. 3.14).

Score reading for classical musicians is an integral part of their training and is a subject studied independently from their instrumental training. Even if a musician does not play in an orchestra, he or she needs to learn to read and "hear" all of the different parts of an orchestra or chamber ensemble score.

Visualizing Music: The Musical Score across the Ages

Score writing, like music, has evolved over the centuries. Looking at scores from the different time zones reveals the growing complexity of representation. The following section includes samples of keyboard, chamber, and orchestral scores from the baroque, classical, romantic, impressionist, and modern time zones. A glimpse at scores from across the centuries reveals what the conductor and the musicians are seeing in performance.

FIGURE 3.14. Beethoven, *Coriolan* Overture.

Not to worry, you can still manage a productive glimpse. You can regard the scores simply as revealing pictures, reflecting some of the major features of the time zone in the designs on the page, and as the historical developments of written music.

- The baroque examples (figs. 3.15 and 3.16): notice the activity, busyness, and repetition of pattern. These scores usually were written in three to five parts for strings and continuo.
- The classical example (fig. 3.17): notice the clear, meticulous, thin nature of the score. With the growth of engraving, musical scores were easier to produce. Often these scores included verbal directions for performance, and some indicated a precise tempo fixed by an early form of the metronome called a *chronometer*. Subdivisions within the various orchestral sections were common. Piracy (producing the music without permission) was common during this time period, especially in France. Dynamics are added to the score, as are phrase lines, articulation markings, and so forth.
- The romantic example (fig. 3.18): notice how the orchestra has grown (twenty-eight staves) and the many more written instructions in the score, indicating a personal directive from the composer. Especially notice the words *molto espr,* meaning "very expressive," or just *espr,* also meaning "expressive." Emotion at this time was very important, and this music was to be played with heart and feeling at the insistent urging of the composer. Score production becomes vastly easier with the invention of lithography. Treatises and primers were written to instruct in the correct method of writing music. The increasing size of the orchestra required greater complexity in the written format. Sometimes metronome markings are indicated, and score writing became subject to individual interpretations of the music, resulting in scores which had been altered from the composer's intent. The source of the score became a very relevant question for performers.
- The impressionist examples (figs. 3.19 and 3.20): notice the sustained tones (the same notes not changing for a long time), the blocks of similar writing, and the shimmering effects (the paired notes with lots of lines under them), creating (when executed) a blurring or mixing of sound which remains static in its direction but vibrating; this technique creates a glowing backdrop or impression.
- The twentieth-century examples (figs. 3.21 and 3.22): obviously, new ideas and explorations are at hand. Even trained musicians will have a hard time with some of these unless conversant with twentieth-century innovations! The larger scores written in conventional notation reflect the complicated nature of certain twentieth-century thought. In the Stravinsky example, you can probably "do the math" to see the dominant rhythmic patterns.

Baroque Musical Score No. 1 (fig. 3.15): J. S. Bach, Fugue 6 from the *Well-Tempered Klavier,* book 2

Key Concepts: fugue form, subject, imitation, contrapuntal texture

Instrumentation: piano, harpsichord or organ; two staves but showing three voices

Fugues were one of the most important baroque forms and textures. In this example the subject entries are marked at the opening.

FIGURE 3.15. Bach, Fugue 6 from the *Well-Tempered Klavier,* book 2.

The order of entry is alto, soprano, and bass, and each entry of the main subject or melodic idea is marked. In fugal writing it was common to have a small "episode," or separation, before the last opening statement of the subject. Since this is a three-voiced fugue, the last opening statement would be the third. "P" represents segments or portions of the theme used in the overall texture but not in complete statements. The second segment reveals a common contrapuntal practice of inversion (marked "I"), turning the theme or part of it upside down. The third segment represents points of imitation, with motifs from the subject.

Baroque Musical Score No. 2 (fig. 3.16): J. S. Bach, *Brandenburg Concerto no. 5*, first movement

Key Concepts: concerto grosso form, imitation, imitative style, contrapuntal texture

Instrumentation: flute, violins, viola, cello, basso continuo played by keyboard

Notice the principal reliance on strings to carry the music. The numbers under the bottom line tell the keyboard player (playing the

FIGURE 3.16. Bach, *Brandenburg* Concerto no. 5, first movement.

basso continuo) what chords to use to fill in the harmony. (See "The Extravagant Baroque, 1600–1750, An Important New Sound: Monody," p. 25.) Despite the thick, dense texture on more staves, the main idea is still imitated sequentially, just as in the fugue.

Classical Musical Score (fig. 3.17): Franz Josef Haydn, Symphony no. 100 in G Major, third movement, "Menuet Moderato"

Key Concepts: clarity, balance, pruning of thickness, mono- or homophonic texture

Instrumentation: flutes, oboes, bassoons, horns, trombones, timpani, violins, violas, celli, and double bass

This example comes from the introduction of the third movement. The instruments are listed on the left-hand side of the score. This line-up is invariable throughout the movement. Each instrument retains the same line throughout the piece. For example, the flutes will retain the top line throughout. If you want to see what the flute is doing all the time, just follow the top line.

Notice that the strings, the backbone of the classical orchestra, have the most important role, but newer instruments such as the oboe have been introduced as well. The basso continuo, counterpoint, and imitation of the baroque have been replaced by the thinner, more carefully ordered sound of the classical.

Also observe the primacy, clarity, and balance of the melodic thought; the theme is presented in the violins, flutes, and oboes, backed by a minimum of accompaniment by the rest of the orchestra.

Now there is increased involvement from the composer in contrast to the baroque scores. You can see this in the time indicator at the top—moderato. Composers were now beginning to specify a relative speed for the piece, as well as specific articulations (such as *pizz* for pizzicato, meaning "plucked strings") and dynamics (such as *f* for forte, meaning "loud," and *p* for piano, meaning "soft").

Romantic Musical Score (fig. 3.18): Richard Strauss, *Don Quixote,* variation 3

Key Concepts: expression, emotion, large orchestral size, program music

Instrumentation: full orchestra, including glockenspiel, harp, timpani, and English horn

The growing complexity in the scores reflects the growing complexity of the music. *Don Quixote* is written for an extremely large orchestra (twenty-eight staves to read at once), with a wide variety of instruments for lavish color. The composer's involvement is intensified through insistence on emotional power and expression, as Strauss offers continuous, specific directions within the music itself. These include tempo instructions (*poco calando,* which means "changing from the preceding," and *im Zeitmass,* meaning "in tempo"); dynamics (diminuendo, pianissimo, piano, crescendos); and specific advice as to expression. For example, *Sehr breit* (meaning "very bright"), *espressivo* and *molto espressivo* ("expressive" and "very expressive"), and *Hervortretend* ("prominently" or "pronounced"). Strauss's instructions extend to individual articulations, such as the long lines over the melody that indicate phrasing.

This tone poem is an example of program music, or music that represents a story or work of art without using a text. Strauss depicts in music the adventures of Don Quixote and his sidekick, Sancho Panza, based on the novel by Cervantes. Each character in the story is represented by a different theme; here, the solo cello (the third stave from the bottom) depicts the don.

Impressionist Musical Score (figs. 3.19 and 3.20): two excerpts from Claude Debussy, *The Sea*

Key Concepts: orchestral textures and instrumental "colors," exotic sound combinations, blurriness in harmony and form

Instrumentation: full orchestra plus two harps

In both excerpts we find certain strong impressionist fingerprints: the tremolo (shaking or rocking back and forth) writing for winds in the first excerpt and the rapidly repeating notes in the strings in the second excerpt. Both effects last for a sustained period of time, and both create the shimmering movement and timbral coloration favored by this school.

FIGURE 3.18. Strauss, *Don Quixote,* variation 3.

FIGURE 3.19. Debussy, *The Sea*, excerpt 1.

FIGURE 3.20. Debussy, *The Sea*, excerpt 2.

In fact, these two passages create an almost static effect; these notes are not "goal-oriented" but create a backdrop to the parts that are in motion (see figure 3.19, number 38, top five lines). In the bottom three lines, the strings are moving in sequenced patterning, creating a sense of distance with the static winds. In the second excerpt, it is the strings that are playing rapidly repeated notes, those repetitions being indicated by the short lines drawn on the note stems. This creates a rather blurred sound against the line in motion (the trumpets), in keeping with the suggestive nature of impressionist music.

Notice as well that Debussy uses two harps. Harps were among the favorite instruments of impressionist composers. The ability of a harp to slide over the notes in long, grand swirls added lush coloration and movement. In the second excerpt, the direction *sur la chevalet* instructs the string players to play near the bridge, the piece of wood which lifts the strings from the instrument. The tone near the bridge is of a special quality from the usual area of bowing and adds to the "exoticism" of the musical sound.

Twentieth-Century Musical Score No. 1 (fig. 3.21): Igor Stravinsky, *The Rite of Spring*

Key Concepts: experimental, unpredictable, innovative rhythms

Instrumentation: full orchestra

Rhythm as a dominant element of music became a feature of certain twentieth-century pieces. Stravinsky's *The Rite of Spring* anticipated that development in a work which rocked and shocked the Western musical world. Its brash, unusual rhythms and beat tampering were potent forecasts of what was to come. This selection, called "The Ritual of Abduction," illustrates certain features of Stravinsky's complicated rhythms and temporal changes.

Here, Stravinsky changes the length and emphasis of the beat by constantly regrouping the notes in shifting combinations. Throughout, the basic time value—the eighth note—remains the same. But the effect is one of constant unpredictability and conflict.

For more, see "The Emancipation of Rhythm" in "The Fragmented Twentieth Century" (p. 61).

FIGURE 3.21. Stravinsky, *The Rite of Spring*, excerpt, "The Ritual of Abduction."

Along with conventional scoring, new types of scores emerged, particularly those written for avant-garde music such as graphic scores, color-coded notation, scores with new notation to represent new sounds (microtones, sound blocks, clusters, etc.), and musique concrète. As *Grove's Dictionary of Music* notes (in "Scores"), "In general, it can be said that the diversity in scores and score-types after 1945 reflects the widespread pluralism of postwar culture."

Since electronic music often does not involve live performers, "notation" is made up of technical instructions involving tape recorders, synthesizers, oscillators (which can produce a fundamental pitch with no harmonics, called sine waves or sawtooth waves, with selected harmonics or triangular waves), mixers, digital filters, and computers. Programming languages moved inevitably into music, and MIDI (musical instrument digital interface) provided a means of performance control for electroacoustic music.

In the twentieth century, score writing for avant-garde and electronic music underwent interesting changes to accommodate the new musical thinking and musical sounds. Notation itself was changed because the old language did not suffice. Organization on the page did not "conform" to the standard pattern described above in the pioneering new field.

Twentieth-Century Musical Score No. 2 (fig. 3.22): George Crumb, *Makrokosmos,* vol. 2, no. 12, "Spiral Galaxy [SYMBOL] Aquarius"

Key Concepts: experimental form, new notation, new sounds from old instruments

Instrumentation: piano

Figure 3.22 is a perfect example of twentieth-century composers "pushing the limits" of conventional notation. Here, the physical score represents the musical concept of the spiral galaxy. Unless the pianist memorized the score, he or she would need a special score rotator (as opposed to a page turner) in performance.

Also notice the unconventional uses of the piano, beginning with the silent depression of the keys. The pianist must reach into the piano to pluck the strings (pizz, or pizzicato) and to drag his fingers over the strings to make a gliss, or glissando. Other special effects include the creation of harmonics, an unusual and eerie piano sound. Other works in the collection ask the pianist to hum, talk, whistle, hiss, or warble as part of the performance, and to use objects such as a thimble when plucking, stroking, or hitting the piano strings.

FIGURE 3.22. Crumb, *Makrokosmos*, vol. 2, no. 12 "Spiral Galaxy [SYMBOL] Aquarius." © 1974 by C. F. Peters Corporation. Used by permission. All rights reserved.

4

CLASSICAL MUSIC SAMPLER

The sampler has been created for you and is based on research done for and notes written for the Indianapolis Symphony Orchestra. The author is grateful for its permission to use this material in *Classical Music Without Fear.*

This *Classical Music Sampler* contains entries from the standard concert repertoire using the following guidelines:

1. representative instrumental works by composers from each of the major musical time zones;
2. works that you are likely to hear in your concert experience; and
3. descriptions which are succinct and accessible.

As the title states, this segment is only *a sampler.* Reasons of space dictated that some major works and composers were excluded that would certainly belong in an expansive review of concert fare. So consider this sampler an appetizer. There are many fine books which discuss concert repertoire exclusively and are, naturally, more inclusive, such as David Ewen's *The Complete Book of Classical Music* and *The World of Twentieth Century Music,* Melvin Berger's *Orchestral Masterpieces,* and D. Kern Holoman's *Evenings with the Orchestra.* In your sampler you will find:

- from the baroque time zone: J. S. Bach; George Frideric Handel; Henry Purcell; Antonio Vivaldi
- from the classical time zone: Ludwig van Beethoven; Franz Joseph Haydn; Wolfgang Amadeus Mozart
- from the romantic time zone: Hector Berlioz; Johannes Brahms; Frédéric Chopin; Antonin Dvořák; Edward Elgar; Cesar Franck; Edvard Grieg; Franz Liszt; Felix Mendelssohn; Modest Mussorgsky; Sergey Rachmaninoff; Nikolay Rimsky-Korsakov; Gioacchino Rossini; Camille Saint-Saëns; Franz Schubert; Robert Schumann; Jean Sibelius; Johann Strauss; Richard Strauss; Pyotr Illich Tchaikovsky; Richard Wagner
- from the twentieth century, including impressionism, avant-garde, and traditional voices: Samuel Barber; Béla Bartók; Leonard Bernstein; John Cage; Elliot Carter; Aaron Copland; Henry Cowell; George Crumb; Manuel De Falla; Claude Debussy; George Gershwin; Charles Ives; Leoš Janáček; Olivier Messaien; Sergey Prokofiev; Maurice Ravel; Silvestre Revueltas; Arnold Schoenberg; William Schuman; Dmitry Shostakovich; Igor Stravinsky

In some cases composers' lives spanned two times zones, as is the case with Sergey Rachmaninoff. In this situation, such composers are placed in the time zone which most accurately reflects their sound and voice. Hence, Rachmaninoff would be placed in the romantic time zone, although his dates are 1873–1943. In some cases, a composer embraces different styles and sounds within his works, and the placement in the aforementioned list is simply arbitrary.

Compiling Your Own Classical Music Collection

It is easy to obtain classical music on CDs. However, the array of choices can be bewildering. To help you make selection decisions for your classical music library, the following points might be helpful.

First: frequently there are multiple recordings of the most famous classical works. It is important for you to buy a "good recording": one that is well recorded, is well played, and presents a good interpretation. How are you to know? Buy a CD which has been recorded by a major symphony orchestra or a well-known, respected conductor or artist.

Second: specialty music shops often have very knowledgeable people on hand to help you with a choice. Do not hesitate to ask the clerk. If you order online, the CD sites often provide snippets of the piece for you to hear and excerpts from reviews.

Third: buy what you like! If you purchase CDs because you feel you "should," chances are, you will not listen to them. If you like Beethoven, for example, zero in on that composer and let others composers wait. Sometimes music stores will allow you to aurally sample the music before buying, and if you have the time, take advantage of that service.

Fourth: access a public or university library for their classical CDs. Their collections usually offer a wide array of choices, and access to them will not cost you a dime!

Fifth: listen to classical music on the radio. You might very well hear something which catches your ear that you would like to own for your collection.

For your consideration, the following sampler list is organized by composers.

Sampler

J. S. Bach (1685–1750)

Brandenburg *Concerti*

In 1721 Bach presented these six concerti to Christian Ludwig, the Margrave of Brandenburg, who had commissioned the works in 1717 while Bach was on a trip to Carlsbad to "take the waters." After receiving the music, the Margrave stashed them in his very large collection of concerti but failed to catalog them. Some reports state that he never listened to them. Under such careless circumstances, it is amazing that these musical gems were not lost. At the disposition of the Margarve's personal goods in 1734, the pieces were discovered and sold. At the very least, at this point they saw the light of day, and under the care of J. P. Kirnberger, Bach's pupil, they were preserved. In 1850 the *Brandenburg* Concerti were published and recognized as masterpieces of baroque music. The six concerti offer a splendid variety of scoring, mood, and content, as well as constituting mature specimens

FIGURE 4.1. Statue of J. S. Bach.
© Dave Bartruff/CORBIS.

of concerto grosso form. This structure pits a small group of instruments (the concertino) with the larger ensemble (the ripieno) and is an ancestor of our modern-day concerto.

Four Orchestral Suites

Sometimes these are called *Ouverturnen,* or overtures. The first term was the one which Bach used. These collections of orchestral dances were written between 1717 and 1750, the year of Bach's death. They offer splendid examples of baroque dances, and their segmented form offers variety and frequent changes of pace.

Samuel Barber (1910–81)

Adagio for Strings *and* Essays for Orchestra

These three works reveal the thoughtful, lyrical style which characterizes the writing of the great American composer Samuel Barber. After September 11 you probably heard the dignified *Adagio* (dating from 1937) many times over: sometimes, it has been called America's national funeral music. It was played at the funerals of President F. D. Roosevelt, Albert Einstein, Princess Grace of Monaco, and President Kennedy, and appeared as background music to the award-winning film *Platoon*. Violins present the main theme, which is shared by the orchestra and builds to a fervent climax before concluding in a quiet, poised restatement of the opening.

The two *Essays for Orchestra* were written between 1937 and '42. The first is lighter and more carefree than the second. These are relatively short and offer fine specimens of Barber's voice.

Béla Bartók (1881–1945)

The Hungarian composer Béla Bartók was one of the most respected and complex twentieth-century composers. He often incorporated Hungarian folk tunes, whole or in part, in his music, rendering a special flavor and unique, colorful inflections. Bartók came to America during the Second World War (in 1940) and lived in extreme poverty and neglect in New York City, where he died in 1945. Ironically, after his death, his music emerged to great acclaim and has remained among the treasures of twentieth-century repertoire.

Suite from The Miraculous Mandarin

This searing musical story (based on the ballet of the same name) focuses on the lives of three thieves (pimps) who force a prostitute to lure men into her room for sex, physical battery, and robbery. Her third "visitor" in this story is a Mandarin who refuses to die in the excitement of watching the girl dance for him. He pursues her with lust and intensity, resisting strangulation and stabbing at the hands of the three men. In the end, as the prostitute seals her mouth on his, the Mandarin finally succumbs in a bloody heap.

Concerto for Orchestra

Not all of Bartók's music is as gripping—or as grim—as *The Miraculous Mandarin*. Concerto for Orchestra offers no grisly scenes and projects some of Bartók's finest orchestral writing. The work was written in 1943 when the frail, eighty-seven-pound composer was consumed by cancer. Encouraged by Serge Koussevitzky and other friends, he managed to rise from his deathbed to produce this stunning work. "The title of this symphony-like orchestral work is explained by its tendency to treat instruments or instrumental groups in a concertante or soloistic manner," Bartók explained in the program notes for the Boston premier. The conception of a concerto for an entire orchestra was Bartók's invention, and this idea became a potent inspiration for future composers. The work requires not only a virtuoso soloist but also a virtuoso orchestra.

Ludwig van Beethoven (1770–1827)

Third Symphony (Eroica)

In 1802 Beethoven stated, "I am not satisfied with my works up to the present time. From today, I mean to take a new road." The road emerged in his Third Symphony.

The Third Symphony opened dramatic changes both in form and content from the preceding poised, classical style. At first Beethoven

Figure 4.2. Bust of Beethoven.
© Hulton-Deutsch Collection/
CORBIS.

dedicated this work to Napoleon, for whom he had utmost respect because of what he believed were Napoleon's sincere revolutionary, democratic ideals. The warrior seemed to be a harbinger of the future. But as Beethoven witnessed Napoleon's ever-expanding ego, climaxing in his assuming the title "emperor" on May 2, 1804, he deleted the original dedication (actually, he tore up the opening page of the manuscript in a rage). "He is nothing but an ordinary mortal!" the composer shrieked. "He will trample all the rights of men under foot to indulge his ambition." Beethoven then changed the dedication to the nonspecific "Sinfonia Eroica, Composed to Celebrate the Memory of a Great Man." The work is generally known simply as the *Eroica,* meaning "of a heroic nature."

The music is painted on a large canvas, is richly orchestrated, and moves beyond classical rules and restraints, offering powerful development of ideas (the development alone is 250 measures, the size of many classical symphonies in their entirety), emotional agitation, and superb craftsmanship of musical thought. Beethoven is now stepping into new territory, courageously speaking in his own voice and opening a new world of musical thinking which would ultimately "revolutionize symphonic music," as Sir George Grove observes. After completing eight symphonies, Beethoven was asked by his poet friend Christoff Kuffner which symphony was his favorite, and he answered simply and without hesitation, the *Eroica.*

Fifth Symphony

The Fifth is possibly the most famous of Beethoven's nine symphonies. It was completed in 1808 and was financed by Beethoven's patron, Count Franz von Oppersdorff. The music reflects, in part, the intensity of Beethoven's life at that time. The composer was fighting impending deafness (the most cruel fate for any musician), Napoleon was marching over his homeland, and his brother had married a "wretched woman" whom the composer dubbed "Queen of the Night." Life at the time of the Fifth Symphony was difficult at best.

The famous motif (ta-ta-ta-TA) opens the symphony and is repeated twice before launching on its vehement musical development. (Legend has it that Beethoven was guided in forming the famous motif

FIGURE 4.3. Beethoven, Fifth Symphony, first movement.

by the chirping of a goldfinch!) The movements following the first are equally communicative and deeply affecting. As the movements unfolded, Beethoven's Fifth Symphony clearly spoke a musical language unheard before. The will, the turbulence, and the insistence of the Fifth were a glimpse into the music yet to come from the master.

Sixth Symphony (Pastoral)

As the subtitle implies, this symphony is about the countryside. Whatever the weather, Beethoven took long walks every day. The Sixth Symphony takes us with him to the nourishing atmosphere in the summer of 1808. Nature was a steady comfort and frequently provided inspiration. "Nature is a glorious school for the heart!" Beethoven wrote in his diary in 1818. After considering five titles, Beethoven selected "Pastoral Symphony, more expression of feeling than painting." The musical scenes are indicated in the title of each movement. Generally the symphony is known simply as the *Pastoral*.

The lyricism of the first movement reflects Beethoven's happiness and contentment in its title, "Awakening Joyful Feelings upon Arrival in the Country." The second movement takes us to a "Scene by the Brook." Wavelike, watery triplet figures murmur through violins and violas, and as the music unfolds, assorted birdcalls are sounded, identifying the composer's favorite birds: a quail (oboe), cuckoos (clarinets), and a nightingale (flute). In the third movement we arrive at a boisterous village festival party. The fourth movement depicts a turbulent storm, and the fifth movement offers "Gladsome and Thankful Feelings after the Storm," in music of spiritual repose and peace.

Seventh Symphony

The rugged, dazzling Seventh Symphony premiered in 1813. Its pulsating music generated wild reactions. Schindler in his 1840 biography of Beethoven remarked that "In regard to the Seventh Symphony the extravagances of this genius have now reached the non plus ultra, and Beethoven must be quite ripe for the madhouse." On June 1, 1815, Beethoven wrote that his Seventh was "a grand symphony and one of my best works." The four movements all project dramatic rhythmic statements, and each includes unforgettable themes etched firmly by the strong pulses. The playfulness of this symphony lies in sharp contrast to Beethoven's life: his deafness was increasing; he was recovering from yet another broken love affair; and Napoleonic attacks were roaring. In spite of these events, Beethoven produced a symphony of energy, strength, and the joy of living.

Piano Concerti

There are five piano concerti. The third, fourth, and fifth are the most frequently performed. Excepting the fifth, all were premiered by Beethoven as pianist.

THIRD PIANO CONCERTO

The Third Piano Concerto, like the Third Symphony, broke new ground. David Ewen assessed, "The Third Concerto was beginning to veer sharply toward new directions. It brought a new independence of thought and motion to the solo instrument; it extended the symphonic breadth of the orchestra; it introduced striking enharmonic passages for the piano." In 1800, this concerto occupied most of Beethoven's composing activity because he was involved with revisions of other pieces and preparation of works for publication. The (confirmed) premier took place in Vienna on April 5, 1803, after several years were spent revising the work. There are three movements: a dramatic first, a serene, exquisite second, and a bright, vigorous, virtuosic conclusion.

FOURTH PIANO CONCERTO

In this work, Beethoven moves the concerto idea into new manifestations. This breathtakingly elegant work was performed only twice in the composer's lifetime, both times with the composer as soloist. Early receptions of the Fourth were not enthusiastic, possibly because of the comparative lack of virtuosic display which audiences of that time craved in a concerto format. "Candidly, I am not a friend of *allegri di bravura* and such since they do nothing but promote mechanism," the composer explained. The concerto simply did not sell and it languished, fading from concert programs for many years. For this reason, sometimes the Fourth was dubbed the *Cinderella* Concerto, as if needing a magical event to restore its life and prominence. Thanks to Mendelssohn, the Fourth Piano Concerto had such an event, emerging under his baton in Leipzig (1836) to an appreciative, enthusiastic reception. After that, the work was never lost to the world again. In its restraint Beethoven bequeathed an important lesson. Concerti do not always have to be a slam-bang affair. A great concerto does not have to be bombastic in showcasing soloistic musicianship and technique in order to leave us enchanted and profoundly impressed.

FIFTH PIANO CONCERTO (*Emperor*)

The massive Fifth Piano Concerto was written in 1809 under very intense circumstances. Napoleon was invading Vienna, and most of the nobility had long since fled the city. But not Beethoven. He wrapped his head in pillows to protect his pained ears from the endless explosions and noise and continued to compose. Somehow his deep artistic commitment explains why he could write in the middle of warfare, surviving under any circumstances. The nickname *Emperor* was assigned by an unidentified publisher, who deemed the title appropriately matching to the grandeur and majesty of the music. "This [was] music of sweeping and imperious grandeur unknown to any concerto written up to 1812 and beside which the dignity of emperors or archdukes loses all consequence," John Burk explained. There are three movements: a massive first movement, which is symphonic in its expanse; the second, which presents a gentle *cantilena* in a hymnlike melody, and is linked by a single note leading to the third and final movement; and the last movement, which erupts into deep rhythmic propulsion and emphatic linear sweeps. Its coda features a duet for piano and timpani and exuberant orchestral writing, which brings the concerto to its close.

Because of the war the premier of the *Emperor* was delayed for two years until 1811 in Leipzig. A Viennese premier followed three months later.

Violin Concerto

Beethoven wrote only one violin concerto, which is often considered one of the finest concerti ever written for the instrument. The premier of the Violin Concerto in 1806 did not present the work in its full glory, and the work barely survived its introduction. Only two days before, the orchestra was unrehearsed and the twenty-six-year-old violin soloist, Franz Clement, was still sight-reading. At the premier concert, the soloist (obviously not taking things too seriously) regaled the audience by inserting one of his own violin compositions, which he played while holding the violin upside down. Early reaction was not totally positive. One contemporary critic, Johann Moser, wrote, "it is to be feared that if Beethoven continues upon this path, he and the public will fare badly." In 1808 Beethoven was encouraged by the noted pianist and composer Muzio Clementi to arrange the concerto for piano and orchestra, perhaps thinking that this would present the concerto in a more favorable light. Like the Fourth Piano Concerto, this work was saved by a later performance (in 1844) when the thirteen-year-old violin prodigy Joseph Joachim played the concerto under the baton of

Felix Mendelssohn. From that time to this, the concerto took its rightful place in the history of Western music as a masterpiece.

Overture to Egmont

The Overture tells a story about the conquering of the Netherlands by the Spanish duke of Alva in the sixteenth century. Like the Third Symphony, this work also is related to Beethoven's defiance of tyranny and his reverence for liberty and equality. The storylike hero of Goethe's tragedy, the count of Egmont, is followed in the music. At the end the count (Lamoral) is beheaded (an impending doom which is forecast at the opening with ominous F-minor chords). Yet, as if in a postscript, the forces of righteousness survive his death, and the work concludes in an exalted section, defying the tyranny of the Spanish forces and indicating the survival of Lamoral's noble spirit and mission.

Hector Berlioz (1803–69)

Symphonie Fantastique

Drugs, murder, and obsession all play a part in the remarkable musical psycho-drama by Hector Berlioz titled *Symphonie Fantastique*. At age twenty-seven, the composer produced a radical work which blazed extraordinary new trails. Audiences of 1830 were used to music which described or represented moods or scenes or even told a story, but the unraveling of a psycho-drama of this nature was astonishing. The massive orchestration and special effects (such as playing with the wooden part of the bow for a skeleton's dance) were stunning, but the graphic unfolding of a pathological love affair was unnerving, at best.

In part, *Symphonie Fantastique* was autobiographical. Berlioz became obsessively smitten by the English actress Harriet Smithson after watching her perform in a traveling Shakespeare company. (He did not speak a word of English, but his passion transcended that hurdle.) For years his letters and entreaties were rebuffed, but eventually he did coax her into marriage. The union was predictably tumultuous and ended in a permanent separation after ten years. After her death Berlioz quickly consoled himself by marrying his mistress.

The stimulus for *Symphonie Fantastique* lay in yet another one of Berlioz's extravagant efforts to get Harriet's attention. He based his symphony on the narrative of De Quincey's *Confessions of an English Opium Eater,* which had been recently translated into French. The plot seemed a perfect match for Berlioz's overheated mental state at the time. At the premier on December 5, notable musicians and composers were in the audience (Liszt, Meyerbeer, and Spontini), but the star of the show, Harriet, was noticeably missing.

Berlioz provided his own program notes in the score to explain *Symphonie Fantastique,* and they began with these words: "A young artist of morbid sensibility and ardent imagination poisons himself with opium in a fit of amorous despair." The overdose creates a series of visions, leading to the dream in which Harriet is murdered and the artist is beheaded, eventually attending his own funeral!

Early on, we are introduced to Harriet (identified by a small musical statement called a "fixed idea"), and she "appears" in all five movements, transforming "herself" according to the situation. The fourth movement depicts the artist's concern that he has killed his beloved and is being led to execution. "March to the Gallows" is singularly intense: solemnity is interrupted with shrieks of joy, as hideous creatures seethe with the pleasure of witnessing a beheading as the accused is led to the guillotine. The fifth movement, titled "Dreams of a Witches' Sabbath," depicts the artist's own funeral with him as an attendee. There the artist is "surrounded by ghosts, sorcerers, and monsters of every kind," according to Berlioz's own program notes, dancing with crazed energy and delight. The witches' dance is a particularly violent orgy, twisting and turning in a fugal texture before church bells chime, prefacing the fiery coda.

Berlioz's music is thrilling at every turn, impeccably orchestrated, and imaginatively conceived. The original scoring called for 220 players, but during his lifetime, Berlioz could only gather approximately 130 musicians for performances of the extraordinary work.

Harold in Italy

The great violinist Paganini was an early admirer of *Symphonie Fantastique,* and a few weeks after the premier he asked Berlioz to write a work for him—featuring the viola (a recent interest). "I have no confidence in anyone but you," Paganini asserted. Early efforts did not please Paganini (he was not playing enough or highlighted enough), and Berlioz walked away from the commission. "Only you can write for yourself," he maintained. At this point, however, the composer was suddenly free to continue as he pleased in writing *Harold in Italy,* a symphony for orchestra with a solo viola.

In four movements, Berlioz describes his own wanderings in the Abruzzi Mountains (a section of the Apennines northwest of Rome) through the character Childe Harold, derived from Byron's poem *Childe Harold's Pilgrimage.* As in *Symphonie Fantastique,* Berlioz creates a "fixed idea" representing the main character, but in this case the fixed idea collaborates with the orchestra and is not disruptive or fearsome. The work premiered on November 23, 1834, and was received with great acclaim. The viola wanders through the score as Harold did in the mountains, and the movements are titled according to the journey and experiences: (1) "Harold in the Mountains: Scenes of Sadness, of Happiness and of Joy"; (2) "March of the Pilgrims Singing Their Evening Prayer"; (3) "Serenade of an Abruzzi Mountaineer to His Mistress"; and (4) "Brigands' Orgy: Memory of Past Scenes."

Leonard Bernstein (1918–90)

Symphonic Dances from West Side Story

The dashing, flashing wunderkind of American music, Leonard Bernstein, created a timeless masterpiece in the musical *West Side Story.* This setting of the dances derived from the show consists of a single movement in nine parts. Cocky, gang-style music alternates with lyrical love themes. The mambo dance competition is particularly cheeky and exciting. No need for staging: this suite tells the whole story in unmistakably graphic musical narrative.

Overture to Candide

Leonard Bernstein worked on his musical *Candide* on and off for thirty years! Some have said it was the most revised work in the history of Broadway. Its sparkling Overture survived all the turbulence and quickly became a stand-alone hit. The Overture is sleek, fast paced, and crammed with melodic delights, and is uninhibited fun— a zippy, witty, sophisticated orchestral romp.

Second Symphony (Age of Anxiety)

This symphony reveals the more serious and complex side of Leonard Bernstein's writing and character. He based the work on W. H. Auden's poem *The Age of Anxiety*. This poem speaks of human insecurity and a search for the constancy and support of an abiding faith. Bernstein began the work in 1947 (writing it in hotel lobbies and "whenever he could get a chance" within his demanding career) and completed it on March 20, 1949. Although the Second Symphony has a serious, passionate intent to stand as absolute music, Bernstein confessed, "I have a deep suspicion that every work I write for whatever medium is really theater music in some way." In 1950 the work was choreographed by Jerome Robbins.

There are six sections grouped into two larger parts, all played without pause, and the composer offered his own notes for the work. Part 1 (prologue) is a kind of symposium on the state of humanity discussed by a girl and three men. "[It is] the loneliest music I know," Bernstein commented. The second part reviews the life of man in a series of variations. The third part continues the variation form.

In part 2, a dirge mourns the loss of a father figure–leader in life. The succeeding masque finds the group in the girl's apartment, determined to "have a party," and the epilogue reveals that what is really enduring in life is faith.

Writing with tremendous craftsmanship and style, Bernstein judiciously references the twentieth-century twelve-tone system, dissonance, polytonality, polyrhythms, and jazz elements, which color the lyricism and illumine the provocative message of Auden's thought.

Georges Bizet (1838–75)

Symphony in C

At age seventeen Bizet (pronounced bee-ZAY) wrote one of the most charming, chipper symphonies in the repertoire. In fact, it was his only symphony. The work lay hidden for some seventy years and finally premiered on February 26, 1935. It is youthful, optimistic, and filled with joie de vivre spun in a classical setting.

Johannes Brahms (1833–97)

Academic Festival Overture

In May 1879 the University of Breslau conferred an honorary doctoral degree upon Johannes Brahms, "recognizing his artistic leadership in Germany of the more severe order." Although Brahms never attended a university, he had spent a lot of time in the university town of Gottinger. That atmosphere provided many student songs which were incorporated into his "thank you" piece for the degree. At first he thought a mere postcard of thanks would suffice, but his friend Bernhard Scholz convinced the composer that a postcard was hardly sufficient!

The *Academic Festival* Overture seemed almost irreverent to mark a *Doctor-symphonie* (a solemn occasion), and it was reported that the audience appeared "considerably shocked" when the jolly piece premiered in Breslau on January 4, 1881. The music is carefree, highlighting student songs, and scored dramatically with a prominent use of trumpets and the inclusion of triangle, cymbals, and piccolo. The very famous student song "Gaudeamus Igitur" (Let Us All Now Enjoy Ourselves) emerges in a grand setting in the final section.

Symphonies

Brahms was known as a traditional composer who resisted the currents of nineteenth-century romantic excesses and "newfangled" forms. He was a composer who was mindful of the heritage of the past and chose to express himself in a more traditional manner than his contemporaries. Yet his voice was unique, powerful, and eminently affecting. His four symphonies reflect that philosophy in their comparative restraint and disciplined formal control.

FIRST SYMPHONY

Brahms's First Symphony emerged when he was forty-three. Although he had toyed with the idea of writing a symphony at age twenty, he waited for two decades before addressing that form. Perhaps Brahms's reverence for Beethoven ("always hearing the master's footsteps behind him") deterred any early attempt. The First Symphony is a dramatic, thrilling work—the product of a composer who has truly found his voice and mastered control of the material. When general listeners commented that the big finale, led off by a hymnlike melody, reminded them of Beethoven's Ninth, Brahms responded, "any fool can see that!"

SECOND SYMPHONY

Like Beethoven's *Pastoral* Symphony, Brahms's Second was inspired by a rural setting. For this reason, it has sometimes been called "Brahms's *Pastoral*." In 1877 Brahms visited the seaside resort of Portschach and during those lighthearted, fun-filled days found the time and stimulus to write his Second Symphony. The village was so filled with music and good melodies that "one must be careful not to tread on them," Brahms wrote. This work is written on a smaller scale than the other three and is often considered the happiest of Brahms's four symphonies.

THIRD SYMPHONY

Brahms's Third Symphony was written in 1883, one year after Brahms had written to his publisher that he was "finished with composing and would never write again." He reversed this course after summering with Hermine Spiess (a twenty-six-year-old contralto) in Wiesbaden. Besides her coaxing him to write again, the promise made by the esteemed conductor Hans von Bulow to have Brahms's new work read by one of Europe's finest ensembles (the Meiningen Orchestra) turned the tide.

The Third was an immediate success at its premier in Vienna on December 2, 1883, and quickly became one of the most famous works.

This is the smallest and most compact of Brahms's four symphonies. There are four movements: the first features a motto figure which uses the notes F-A-F. The distinctive motif was, as explained by the composer, to mean *Frei aber Froh* (free but happy). The writing is rich, dramatic, and intense. The second movement offers splendid wind writing and many references to the F-A-F motto derived from the opening movement. The third features a very tender melody sung by the cello which appears after a melancholy introductory waltz. The fourth movement resumes the grandeur of the first in opulent, grand statements packed with emotion, yet never released into romantic exuberance. "In der Beschrankung seigt sich der Meister" (Restraint is the mark of a master), Brahms commented.

FOURTH SYMPHONY

Brahms's final symphony was composed during two summers the composer spent in the resort town of Murzzuschlag, Austria, in 1884 and 1885. "It is questionable whether I will ever expose the public to the piece," Brahms stated after a four-hand version was received with only mild approval. However, as in the case of the Third Symphony, the composer changed his mind. This time, however, he upstaged Hans von Bulow at the premier in an event that was so successful von Bulow resigned his post in a jealous rage. That friendship was broken for years. Undeterred by the tantrum, Brahms immediately proceeded to take the Meiningen Orchestra on a nine-city tour, featuring, of course, the Fourth Symphony. Audiences were delighted, often clapping so hard that certain movements had to be repeated on the spot!

The symphony is massive, and its four stunning movements reflect a lifetime of musical creativity and emotion. At the last orchestral concert which Brahms attended in his life, this was the symphony he heard. It was observed that he cried throughout.

Piano Concerti

Brahms wrote two piano concerti, twenty-two years apart. In 1854, Brahms wrote to his friend Robert Schumann that he was "starting a symphony." A projected two-piano work in D minor was giving him fits, and the composer decided that the material might do better in a symphonic setting. This did not work either. Finally, after conferring with the great violinist Joseph Joachim, he decided that reworking the ideas into a piano concerto would be the answer. After an off-and-on process of five years, the concerto was completed in the summer of 1859, with Robert Schumann's wife, Clara, as the soloist. The premier in Leipzig was a disaster. Audiences hissed. Michael Roeder assessed: "That Leipzig concert proved to be the greatest artistic disaster of Brahms' career." This negative response is perhaps one reason that Brahms did not write another piano concerto until 1881. History has reversed the early assessment, and the First Piano Concerto now ranks as one of the great piano concerti in the repertoire.

The concerto's first movement is filled with intensity, opening with a bold orchestral lightning strike and thundering kettledrums. The turbulence continues until the entry of the soloist. The piano's opening melody is marked legato and piano (smooth and quietly), an about-face from the roar of the beginning. From that point forward, the movement unfolds with potent lyricism and drama. Brahms once noted that the second movement was a "portrait of Clara Schumann"; however, on the first page of the score is the statement, "Blessed is he who comes in the name of the Lord." Some have conjectured that the movement was a response to Schumann's death. The music herein is intimate and profound. A seven-part rondo, led off by the piano, opens the finale, and the concerto springs to life as a brilliant nineteenth-century showpiece.

Describing the Second Piano Concerto, Brahms wrote to a friend, "I have written a tiny piano concerto with a tiny wisp of a scherzo." The tease actually referred to one of the most monumental works in the literature. The concerto is in four movements, rather than the traditional three, wherein Brahms inserts a scherzo between the first and second movements. The first movement opens with an introductory conversation between piano and horn, after which the piano leaps into a demanding cadenza. After this, an orchestral tutti presents the two main contrasting ideas. The music evolves steadily into a huge development, referencing the opening horn call. A traditional recapitulation is capped by a strong coda. The scherzo maintains the energetic mood, and the piano and orchestra collaborate in a rhythmically vivacious interplay. The concerto calms itself in the slow andante movement, focusing on a melody sung by a solo cello which is shared by violins and solo piano. Within this a bristling middle section revives the opening vigor but ultimately yields to a recall of the opening tenderness in a dialogue between clarinets and soloist at the close. The finale bounces from the piano, retaining the opening vigor in a jolly skipping-tune which seems to fertilize more vivacious melodies. As the music unfolds, momentum, complexity, and vast orchestral color are unstoppable. At all times, the piano sparkles with bright passagework, performing technical feats of dash and daring before the orchestra surges into an enormous final crescendo. Brahms completed the massive work in May 1881 and was soloist at the world premier in Budapest on November 9, 1881.

Distinguished, dazzling interpretations of both these concerti are rendered in recordings by the great American pianist Andre Watts.

Frédéric Chopin (1810–49)

After age twenty-one, Frédéric Chopin focused entirely on music for the piano until his death at age thirty-nine. More than any other composer he showcased the piano and reveled in its potential. Chopin composed as he played: with refinement and with emphasis on lyrical projection while spinning intricate, elaborate melodic structures colored by luxuriant harmonies. An extraordinary pianist himself, Chopin always wrote music which "lies well under the hand." He was one of the first composers to indicate fingerings for his music, convinced that different fingers produced different sounds. Subtleties of this type abound in his music, and his repertoire and playing were most beautifully displayed in smaller venues such as Parisian salons rather than in large concert halls. Therein his suave lyric beauty and intimate voice left a bewitching, beguiling legacy. Socially, he was an *homme charmant,* a darling of Parisian society (where he lived from 1832 to '48), a close friend to musicians, poets, Polish exiles, and wealthy families.

Often called the "poet of the piano," Chopin bequeathed an enormous repertoire which includes scherzos, rondos, impromptus, variations, etudes, preludes, waltzes, mazurkas, ballades, nocturnes, sonatas, and two concerti. All have become an integral part of the canon of Western piano music. David Ewen has summarized, "His music is so thoroughly pianistic that it cannot be conceived in terms of any other instrument. . . . He revolutionized piano technique. . . . He created an epoch in piano music. Indeed it is not too much to say that modern piano music and modern piano technique began with Chopin."

Chopin excelled in and focused on smaller forms, although distinguished works in larger dimensions such as the ballades, late sonatas, F Minor Fantasy, Andante Spianato and Polonaise, and two concerti speak of interest in larger forms from time to time. Approximately one-fourth of Chopin's piano repertoire consists of music for the dance. In this area, there are three basic segments: dramatic waltzes, fervent mazurkas, and polonaises. His dances are often brilliant,

JOHN CAGE

John Cage felt that Western music had finally run its course, and that American composers needed to find a refreshing new beginning through utilizing new media and methods for creating music. "I am devoted to the principles of originality," he explained (see "The Fragmented Twentieth Century," p. 58). Examples of this thought are his *Imaginary Landscape No. 3* (1942) for percussion, which includes electronic and mechanical devices such as variable speed turntables, a buzzer, and frequency oscillators to provide the musical stuffing. *Imaginary Landscape No. 4* presents twelve radios, with two performers per radio switching the stations and regulating the volume. "This composition consequently consists of an indeterminate amalgamation of music, speech, radio static, squeals . . . and silence," David Ewen explained. Cage's *Three Dances for Two Prepared Pianos* (a piano stuffed with nuts, screws, clothespins, bolts, etc. in its strings, thereby changing the pitch and sound quality) will give you a taste of his experimentation in this area; it has been recorded on CD by Attacca.

ELLIOT CARTER

Elliot Carter is an American composer known for his "intellectual" approach to music, often writing music of enormous complexity. A special interest is in rhythms which combine both horizontally and vertically and in musical textures. Despite his decidedly cerebral orientation, Carter writes music which is filled with tenderness, powerful climaxes, and a certain mystery. He has received two Pulitzer Prizes, a Gold Medal from the National Institute of Arts and Letters, and many other major prizes and commissions. He has an extended discography that includes Concerto for Orchestra, *Night Fantasies for Piano,* and Concerto for Piano, which are good starting points.

HENRY COWELL

Henry Cowell created a new sound for music through tone clusters. Usually chords and harmonies are built of intervals of a third, but Cowell changed the building blocks to smaller units of a second, yielding a totally different sound in tone combinations. Sometimes these special chords were iterated by banging the forearm or fist on the piano keyboard. Aptly he titled his first effort in this direction "Adventure in Harmony." CDs of Henry Cowell's music such as *Sound Forms for Piano, Piano Music,* and *Gay American Composers* will provide an introduction for you. He also investigated American rural hymnology and Asian music, and his investigations into these areas were significant explorations in American music of the twentieth century.

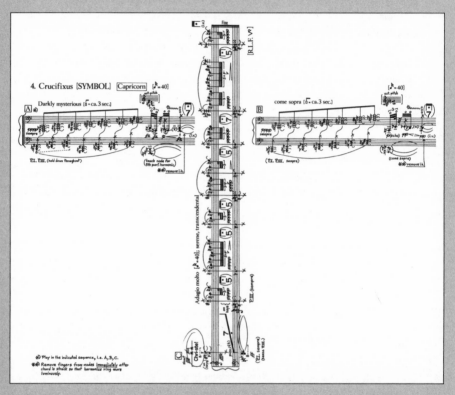

FIGURE 4.4. Crumb, *Makrokosmos*, vol. 2, no. 4 "Crucifixus [SYMBOL] Capricorn." © 1974 by C. F. Peters Corporation. Used by permission. All rights reserved.

GEORGE CRUMB

George Crumb offers music filled with well-defined solo lines, dramatic silences, and blending of voices and instruments as well as explorations into tuning to create (in his words) "special pungency." He is American trained and currently is professor emeritus at the University of Pennsylvania. Theatrical moments abound in his music. In *The Voice of the Whale,* for example, he asks the musicians to wear masks and perform under a blue light (thereby creating a sense of the ocean). His scores are often unique as well, and sometimes his music is written on a circular staff. In 1968 he won a Pulitzer Prize for his *Echoes of Time and the River.*

A significant discography is available for George Crumb. Within this, *A Complete Crumb Edition: Makrokosmos I and II* (for amplified piano) and *Sonic Encounters: The New Piano, Voice of the Whale and Black Angels* (an amplified string quartet which includes the unique sound of bowing water goblets) are good starting points. His vocal music sometimes asks the performer to sing through a cardboard tube or to shout, laugh, and sigh—thereby using the human voice in very novel ways. Crumb's *Ancient Voices of Children* is particularly notable for its unusual settings of excerpts of poetry by García Lorca. "I feel that the essential meaning of his poetry is concerned with the most primary things: life, death, love, the smell of the earth, the sounds of the wind and the sea," he stated.

If you do not wish to commit to a single composer in this experimental area of twentieth-century music, a CD entitled *Pulse* will offer a nice collection of music by John Cage, Henry Cowell, Harvey Sollberger, Lukas Foss, and Lou Harrison.

Zeitgeist (founded in 1977) is a group which has extensively recorded contemporary music, and The First Avenue Ensemble (a trio founded in 1982) is another group which offers reliable performances.

always engaging, and filled with captivating melodies. The nocturnes provide contrast in their quieter, reflective mood and are usually written in a basic ABA format (the B section offering a vivacious contrast before the gentler A section resumes). Virtuosity abounds in the flashing polonaises, scherzos, and etudes, while the preludes offer a wide variety of moods and technical demands in small formats.

A beginning Chopin sampler would include: the Preludes, the Nocturnes, the Waltzes, and the Polonaises.

Aaron Copland (1900–90)

Aaron Copland is one of the most treasured, distinguished, and representative American composers. In his autobiography *Composer from Brooklyn,* Copland wrote of his early desire to write music that would be immediately "recognized as American in character." In the course of his illustrious career he did exactly that.

During the years of World War II the composer focused much of his composing effort on serving the United States, writing works of a patriotic nature. *Preamble for a Solemn Occasion, Lincoln Portrait, Fanfare for the Common Man,* and the *Twelve Poems of Emily Dickinson* speak to that commitment. In 1950 and 1952 he wrote two collections of *Old American Songs,* culling tunes from early America.

Appalachian Spring

Copland's music for *Appalachian Spring* (ballet and suite) displays a springtime wedding celebration around a new farmhouse in the Pennsylvania hills in the early part of the twentieth century. The evocative music takes us to the wedding, reveals the feelings of bride and groom, reflects the celebration, and closes with the final quiet moments when the couple are left alone in their new house. The music is folklike, informal, shimmering like spring, and endearing as the subject. The work won the Pulitzer Prize for music in 1945, the same year in which Copland arranged an orchestral suite derived from the ballet.

El salón México

After two visits to Mexico (in 1932 and 1936), the composer was so captivated by the sounds of Mexican song and dance that in 1937 he produced a remarkable musical memory, *El salón México.* "If you have ever been in Mexico you probably know why a composer should want to write a piece about it," Copland wrote.

The Salon Mexico was a nightclub and dance hall that featured "a grand Cuban orchestra" and three distinct halls, one reserved for those who were barefoot! Copland visited the Salon Mexico on many occasions and credited those times with the raison d'être of his work. ("My piece might never have been written if it hadn't been for the existence of the Salon Mexico," he stated.) Catchy Latin American rhythms, big band scoring, and Mexican popular tunes all blend in a rousing tribute to America's southern neighbor.

Music for the Movies

In 1942 Aaron Copland synthesized a five-movement suite derived from his film scores. "I dedicated the work to Darius Milhaud, whom I consider a pioneer in the field of film music," Copland declared. The suite contains music from *The City, Of Mice and Men,* and *Our Town.* Other film scores also coming from his pen are those for *The North Star* (1943), *The Cummington Story* (1945), *The Red Pony* (1948), *The Heiress* (1948), and *Something Wild* (1961).

Third Symphony

In 1943 Copland was commissioned by the Koussevitzky Foundation for a symphony. The Third Symphony includes themes he had collected for many years. "Inevitably the writing of a symphony brings with it the question of what it is meant to express. I suppose if I forced myself I could invent an ideological basis for my symphony. But, if I did, I would be bluffing. One aspect of the symphony ought to be pointed out: it contains no folk or popular materials. Any reference to jazz or folk material in this work was purely unconscious," he explained.

Copland provided notes for all four movements. The symphony reveals the depth of Copland's skills and talents, demonstrating his ability to work in one of the most difficult and traditional musical vehicles. The themes are beautifully crafted and brilliantly displayed in imaginative orchestration.

Music for the Theatre

"During the late twenties it was customary to pigeonhole me as a composer of symphonic jazz with emphasis on the jazz. More recently I have been catalogued as a purveyor of Americana!" Copland commented in his notes to the Third Symphony. That American voice is captured succinctly and unmistakably in his lighthearted *Music for the Theatre* (1925). This work is a suite in five movements filled with the various inflections and sounds of American jazz and blues.

Claude Debussy (1862–1918)

Prelude to "The Afternoon of a Faun"

It is hard to believe that a work as delicate and tender as *Prelude to "The Afternoon of a Faun"* lobbed a musical grenade. Edward Downes wrote that "Debussy must be the gentlest revolutionary who ever attacked an ancient establishment structure and brought it thundering down around the ears of his frightened contemporaries—while he acted the innocent bystander, claiming (only) that he disliked loud noises." The premier of this groundbreaking piece was at the Société Nationale de Musique on December 22, 1894. At that time, it was performed twice.

Debussy's work takes its title from a poem by the symbolist poet Mallarmé. The music is a "free illustration of the scenes in the poem," the composer explained. A solo flute begins singing an undulating, sinuous theme. The meandering, melodic line immediately forecasts a very new declamation. Throughout the piece rhythms are softened, and dreamy orchestration continues the quiet allure. Lush blending of sounds and careful highlighting of individual timbres result in a work which illustrate in its suggestive evanescent style the major tenets of musical impressionism.

The Sea

Debussy, the great impressionist composer, had a lifelong admiration and love for the sea. "The sea is always endless and beautiful. It is really the thing in nature which best puts you in your place. . . . The sea has been very good to me. She has shown me all her moods. . . . You do not know perhaps that I was intended to the fine career of a sailor and that only the chances of life led me away from it. . . . I have an endless store of memories." In fact, however, the only times Debussy was ever on the ocean were tiny trips on the English Channel!

Nonetheless, Debussy had internalized enough impressions to write a musical triptych in *The Sea* (see score excerpts, figs. 3.19 and 3.20). Water was an alluring image for impressionist composers. The first sketch is titled "From Dawn until Noon on the Sea." The description of dawn and the powerful ocean open the music, and with the climactic brass entrance one can envision and feel the brilliance of high noon streaking across the water. The second sketch, which continues without pause from the first, is titled "The Play of the Waves." Again, as in the first section, the music opens quietly and grows into a brilliant scherzo as the waves tumble over one another. Beguiling writing for winds is one of the great hallmarks of the French school, and the writing for them in this section is stunning. The third sketch is titled "Dialogue of the Wind and Sea." A distant storm roars to the forefront and stirs the ocean into an immense fury before an exquisite melody emerges to divert the frenzy. The wildness resumes, leading to a huge climax before *The Sea* closes with rocking figures recalling the movement of the waves.

The Sea's debut was engulfed in a scandal involving Debussy's relationship with Emma Bardac, the wife of a Parisian banker. Neither Bardac nor Debussy had bothered to get divorces after moving in together in 1905; at the premier of *The Sea,* Bardac was very pregnant and she delivered Debussy's daughter two weeks later. That scandal was running high and perhaps was a distracting current to undivided musical attention. Parisians were itching to punish. One reviewer (Pierre Lalo) in a self-righteous pique commented, "I neither hear nor see nor feel the sea." The evocation of the sea is nonetheless unmistakable, and Debussy's masterpiece, now long separated from the scandal, has since that time left us spellbound.

Manuel De Falla (1876–1946)

Nights in the Gardens of Spain

Nights in the Gardens of Spain is a tripartite orchestral evocation of Spain. According to De Falla, the work is "more expressive than descriptive." The large piano part in this work stems from the original concept, which was for piano solo. Later, the conception was revised to include orchestra; the decision was a good one. De Falla was a master of evocative orchestration, and in this piece the lavish instrumental color adds a vibrant dimension to the scenes. Themes, rhythms, and ornamental figures are frequently generated from popular Andalusian music, thereby creating a very authentic sound. The three nocturnal pictures were composed between 1909 and 1915. The final two are linked via a tremolo bridge in the violins.

The first garden is titled "In the Generalife," a setting in one of the outlying buildings connected with the Alhambra. The second garden is titled "Dance in the Distance," and in this case the garden was not identified. As W. R. Anderson commented, "About us again are the orange trees, the myrtles and the palms, the splashing waters. Mandolins and guitars play scraps of oriental-sounding tunes, coming nearer in the gentle wafts of tones upborne, now falling on the light breeze." The third nocturne is titled "In the Gardens of the Sierra de Cordoba." Anderson continues his description, saying, "We may well feel like the sleeper awakened in the *Arabian Nights* for we seem to hear and see with sense other than our own while yet we know we do not merely dream. It is one of the finest romantic explorations of our day." It is also one of the most beautiful examples of musical impressionism in the repertoire.

Antonin Dvořák (1841–1904)

Ninth Symphony (From the New World)

Antonin Dvořák was a master of nationalistic writing, that is, music which evokes a particular country or its culture. He loved America, and when he summered in Spillville, Iowa, he enthusiastically attended Buffalo Bill's Wild West shows! After spending three years in New York (1892–95), he was fascinated by and appreciated American culture but became exceedingly concerned about the lack of truly American-sounding music. In his opinion, black spirituals and the songs and dances of American Indians were a fertile legacy for American musical thought. As he stated, "I am convinced that the future of music in this country must be founded on what are called Negro melodies. These can be the foundation of a serious and original school of composition to be developed in the United States. When I first came here, I was impressed with the idea, and it has [now] developed into a settled conviction. These beautiful and varied themes are a product of the soil. Your composers must turn to them. . . . In the Negro melodies of America I discover all that is needed for a great and noble school of music." Dvořák's friendship with a black composition student named Harry Burleigh was a primary source for his exposure to black spirituals.

His Ninth Symphony, subtitled *Symphony from the New World*, resonated with Americans, becoming so famous that Dvořák became a household name. At that time, Americans were thrilled that a famous, world-class composer would find their music and its style respectable. Dvořák's interest and endorsement legitimized their native music. "That our national identity in music should be more linked to the New World Symphony than to music composed by Americans simply shows how tied to our European lineage we were," Jonathan Kramer observed.

The first movement of the Ninth Symphony reveals Dvořák's convictions about American native music by quoting the famous melody "Swing Low, Sweet Chariot," which was one of Dvořák's favorite American spirituals. The second movement contains a theme played by the English horn which bears a strong kinship to American folk music, and which was later used by William Arms Fisher for his text "Goin' Home." The third movement emerges with a bright scherzo, perhaps referencing Indian dances (or even perhaps Czech peasants). The fourth movement is a massive conclusion to the symphony, recalling themes from previous movements but basically concerning itself with the triumphant theme proclaimed by horns and trombones at the opening.

Edward Elgar (1857–1934)

Enigma Variations

You are probably acquainted with one of Elgar's most famous pieces, derived from the "Pomp and Circumstance" marches, as it is played at many graduations. (That familiar piece is the first of the set of five noble marches written between 1901 and 1930.) The nobility of the first march is a hallmark of Elgar's richly orchestrated, refined music.

One of his most original and interesting works is *Enigma Variations*. Thirteen variations were written to capture and honor personal friends of the composer, which explains the (personal) initials supplied by Elgar preceding the sections. The fourteenth variation is a musical self-portrait. Herein you will meet (in order) the composer's wife, a pianist friend (indicated by all the scales), a bass singer (whose voice is represented by the bassoon), an elegant country squire, a very funny storyteller, a beautiful violin student (listen for the violin exercises and beautiful tune), an architect who was prone to say the unexpected (hence the music is surprising), a gracious secretary, a musicologist, a close friend, a friend's rejoicing over a dog who was saved from the river, a cellist, an undisclosed lady (probably Lady Mary Lygon) who was on a sea voyage when he was composing *Variations,* and Elgar himself.

César Franck (1822–90)

Symphonic Variations for Piano and Orchestra

César Franck ultimately became one of the most esteemed French composers, but his fame came late in life—in his sixties. Some have said that he took longer than almost any other composer to come to musical maturity. Most of his unheralded life he was known as a gentle organ teacher. His character was so endearing and kind that he was sometimes called "Father Franck." Then in his last five years, the quiet, unassuming gentleman launched three outstanding major works: the Piano Quartet, *Three Chorales for Organ,* and *Symphonic Variations for Piano and Orchestra.*

This one-movement work is one of the most luxuriant, vast, and colorful nineteenth-century romantic pieces. In *Symphonic Variations,* Franck perfectly meshes the piano and orchestra in a single unit rather than separating soloist from ensemble as one might find in a concerto. Unlike *Enigma Variations* discussed above, and most variations for that matter, there is no sharp partitioning, as is found in more customary variation procedure; the work is a single piece.

George Gershwin (1898–1937)

Rhapsody in Blue

George Gershwin was one of American's most beloved composers. His music dominated Broadway theaters during the 1920s and 1930s, sweeping into American hearts and psyches. Gershwin's songs resonated with American culture and attitudes. Collaboration with his brother, Ira, resulted in a magical combination. George Gershwin also had a significant presence outside of the Broadway scene. Leonard Bernstein noted that he was eager "to cross over to the other side of the tracks" and enter the world of serious music (an early cross-over composer!). A malignant brain tumor claimed his life at age thirty-eight. Upon his early death, Arnold Schoenberg commented, "I do not know whether history will consider Gershwin a kind of Johann Strauss, or Debussy, Offenbach, or Brahms, Lehar, or Puccini. But I do know he is an artist and a composer, he expressed musical ideas, and they were new, as in the way in which he expressed them." His pioneering blend of jazz and classical style became a landmark in the history of American music. His *Rhapsody in Blue* was not only a stunning work but also a significant prophecy for the future.

Rhapsody was written upon request from Paul Whiteman for a concert which was "to display American music in all its major facets." Gershwin decided to write a jazz concerto. As the composer explained, "In the *Rhapsody,* I tried to express our manner of living, the tempo of our modern life with its speed and chaos and vitality."

The work opens with the famous clarinet slide, which actually began as a long trill, but the clarinetist decided to just slide to the top at a rehearsal to avoid articulating each note. Gershwin loved the change and let it stand. Melodies in *Rhapsody* run the gamut of jazzy to sentimental to serious, and the music is colored by the insertions of "blue notes" and catchy rhythms with shifting accents. The work deservedly has become an American classic.

An American in Paris

Gershwin's tone poem is a description of a visit to Paris; it is filled with the exuberance of being in that magical city, and wisps of nostalgia and memories of home are woven into this exhilarating score. The work captures the excitement of an American upon arriving in the city, and includes walking-like tunes indicating his strolling, taxicab horns, a blues song (memories of home), and a jubilant finale. The title was used for a movie in 1951 which received an Academy Award, starring Gene Kelly and Leslie Caron. Gershwin's score was also used in the famous ballet danced by Kelly and Caron.

Variations on "I Got Rhythm"

Ethel Merman's famous song, which launched her to stardom in *Girl Crazy,* became the topic for this set of variations for piano and orchestra. The work is filled with jazzy rhythms, snappy variations, and pungent blues.

Edvard Grieg (1843–1907)

Piano Concerto in A Minor

One of the loveliest piano concerti in the repertoire came from the Norwegian composer Edvard Grieg. He was often noted for his lyricism, his "Norwegian sound" resulting from his inclusion of folk music and folk inflections in his musical expression. The piano concerto is one of his finest and most tuneful works. Its enduring popularity rests in part because of its "easy listening" quality, its toe-tapping, dancelike rhythms, and its beautiful melodies—as well as for its exquisite writing for the piano.

George Frideric Handel (1685–1759)

George Frideric Handel was one of the great stars of the baroque period. He eventually settled in England, where he became a beloved, revered, and welcomed guest. The queen even gave him a yearly stipend, and Handel decided to stay, much to the annoyance of his Austrian employer, the elector of Hanover. Later, this same elector became George I of England! Fortunately for Handel, King George I did not harbor a grudge against Handel, whose oratorio the *Messiah* remains his most famous composition.

Royal Fireworks *Music and* Water Music

Handel was well known and acclaimed during his lifetime and was a prolific composer in many fields. When the English king asked for some music to celebrate peace after the War of Austrian Succession, he stated he "wanted no fiddles." Handel obliged at first, and *Royal Fireworks* called for a large orchestra of winds, brass, kettledrums, and a contrabassoon. The idea was to "outshine" the upcoming celebratory fireworks. Later versions did include strings, however. Twelve thousand people attended the early rehearsal of the majestic,

FIGURE 4.5. Thomas Hudson, portrait of Handel. By
courtesy of the National Portrait Gallery, London.

thrilling new work in Vauxhall Gardens. At the official event, held on
April 27, 1749, Handel's music easily outdid the projected spectacle.
Many of the rockets would not light, and the scaffolding from which
the fireworks were to have been launched caught fire itself and burned
to the ground. There are six parts to the piece: the energetic overture;
a bright bourrée (dance); a suave, serene section acknowledging peace;
a bright section featuring the trumpet; a contrasting minuet (dance);
and a concluding minuet.

During Handel's time, it was a popular custom to have barges of musicians float up and down the Thames River in the summer to provide music for "water concerts." There are three popular sets of *Water Music,* which are compilations of various pieces that Handel wrote for these unique concerts. The music is tuneful, enjoyable, and eminently accessible, having been written for lighthearted events.

Franz Joseph Haydn (1732–1809)

Franz Joseph Haydn was one of the major composers of the classical period. He is sometimes known as the creator of the string quartet, and his writings in the symphonic field were foundational in the structure of the Viennese classical symphony. For thirty years he worked as Kapellmeister at the Count of Esterházy's lavish estates, particularly Esterháza, on the outskirts of Vienna. The count offered Haydn living space (in the stables) and provided an orchestra and the opportunity and time to compose. Music was in high demand at the estates, and every day (according to contemporary reports) there were musical performances, always attended by Prince Esterházy himself. If a special guest arrived, new music to honor his or her presence was also required. Haydn seized this employment opportunity with gusto and served the prince well. During his employment with the prince, he wrote approximately eighty symphonies and divertimenti and forty string quartets, operas, concerti, and solo instrumental works. Possibly he wrote voraciously to escape the nagging of a most unpleasant wife, who used to cut up his manuscripts for hair curlers!

Part of the appeal of Haydn's genial music is the incorporation of delightful folk tunes (emanating perhaps from his fascination with Croatian folk songs), and he was one of the first composers to incorporate "popular" music into serious art forms. Haydn's love of life, his endearing character and sentiment, and his exquisite craftsmanship are found in every aspect of his writing. Because he was so lovable and generous, he was sometimes called "Papa Haydn" by his contemporaries.

Symphonies

Many of Haydn's symphonies are titled. For your enjoyment, I would suggest:

- No. 31, *Hornsignal* Symphony (named for the horn calls incorporated in the work)
- No. 45, *Farewell* Symphony (musicians leave the stage to indicate a good-bye to the count when he would not agree to have them return to Vienna for some time off during their summer duties at his country estate)
- No. 83, *Hen* Symphony
- No. 85, *Queen* Symphony (supposedly Marie Antoinette's favorite symphony)
- No. 92, *Oxford* Symphony (written when Haydn received a doctor's degree from that university)
- No. 94, *Surprise* Symphony (the "surprise" is a very loud chord occurring in the quiet theme of the andante movement)
- No. 100, *Military* Symphony (named after the military nature of the second movement; see fig. 3.17 for an excerpt)
- No. 101, *Clock* Symphony (named after the second movement's tick-tock rhythm)
- No. 103, *Drumroll* Symphony (named after the solo drumroll with which the symphony begins)

Charles Ives (1874–1954)

Charles Ives is one of America's most interesting composers. His father had been a bandmaster in the Civil War, and as a musician himself, started Charles's music training early. The youngster was innovative from the beginning, and he frequently turned away from the standard hymn tunes, Bach, and traditional harmonies, which were his father's staples in music training, in order to discover new, more exciting sounds. An understanding pastor, Ralph Griggs, supported the youngster's experiments, saying, "God must get awfully tired of hearing the same thing over and over. . . . He would certainly embrace a dissonance . . . and might even positively enjoy one now and then."

Ives was precocious in music but did not want to rely on music for a livelihood. Of all things, he turned to insurance, and he even founded his own firm, which, by the time he retired, had become the largest insurance agency in the United States!

Music remained with him nonetheless, and he became an American composing pioneer. However, his unique sounds and daring innovations resulted in music which was not heard for long periods of time.

FIGURE 4.6. Charles Ives. © Bettmann/CORBIS.

Conductors did not want to take a chance. The Third Symphony, subtitled *The Camp Meeting,* won a Pulitzer Prize in 1947—after having lain dormant for forty-three years. The esteemed composer and conductor Gustav Mahler did find the cheeky composer interesting and had plans to conduct the famous Third Symphony in Europe as well as America, but the plan was stopped by the conductor's untimely death. Leopold Stokowski was another conductor fascinated by Ives's ingenuity and the well-crafted nature of Ives's thinking. His championship of Ives's last symphony, the Fourth, was critical in establishing Ives's respectability.

Three Places in New England

Ives's musical triptych is firmly anchored in the United States. The titles of the movements provide his musical itinerary as Ives takes listeners to St. Gaudens in Boston Common (section 1), portraying Colonel Shaw and his Colored Regiment; to Putnam's Camp, Redding, Connecticut (section 2); and to the Housatonic at Stockbridge (section 3). Polyrhythms (several rhythms played simultaneously) and polytonality (several keys played at once) create a very modern sound in all the sections.

The first section describes emotions attendant to the Civil War and offers American-style tunes reminiscent of that time. In the second section, a Fourth of July picnic is portrayed at Putnam's Camp, a small park which was the winter quarters of General Putnam's soldiers in 1778–79. Ives's portrayal of two bands approaching simultaneously from different directions is a particularly graphic and unforgettable moment. Nicolas Slonimsky (who conducted the premier in 1931 with the Boston symphony) once described this section as a *"musicorama* of the American Revolution," with its quotes from revolutionary songs and marches. The Housatonic is a river in Stockbridge, Massachusetts. At first the music depicts the river flowing serenely, then enters into a strong turbulent climax as the water churns, and finally relaxes as the river subsides. In a concluding section, a solo violin sings in a rhythm quite different from the ensemble and provides harmonic clashes as well, continuing the polytonal and polyrhythmic features of the preceding sections.

Leoš Janáček (1854–1928)

Sinfonietta

Janáček's (pronounced YA-na-check) bright Sinfonietta will give you a quick sample of his unique, passionate musical voice. The character of Janáček's music derives largely from his use of Moravian folk tunes and the rhythms of the Czech language, transcribed into his music. "I am certain that all melodic and rhythmic mysteries in general are to be explained solely from rhythmical and melodic points of view on the basis of melodic curves of speech," he commented.

The Sinfonietta began as a set of brass fanfares which were later transcribed into a five-movement suite. The work is brisk, energetic, and bursting with rhythmic folk tunes and unstoppable high spirits.

Franz Liszt (1811–86)

Liszt's life and career were marked by extravagant behavior, turbulence, controversy, pioneering musical innovations in form and harmony, and intellectual brilliance. On the one side, there was Liszt the dazzling piano virtuoso, "rock-star" performer, swashbuckling ladykiller, facile showman, and man of the world who had many affairs.

On the other side was Liszt the serious composer, deeply religious in spirit (he became an abbé of the Third Order of St. Francis of Assisi), creator of the symphonic tone poem, a generous teacher, and a conductor. These contradictory elements were inextricably welded in Liszt, one of the most innovative and influential composers of the nineteenth century. His music reflects this duality—sometimes it is all flash and dash; at other times it soars to the highest beauty and spirituality. It just depends on which Liszt is speaking.

The success of Liszt's colorful tone poems fostered an entire genre of nineteenth-century music. In a tone poem, an extramusical concept such as a story, a poem, an idea, or an emotion is expressed in music. That outside source determines the musical focus and provides logical coherence. Liszt would have agreed with Ernst Toch who wrote that "in any narrative—epic, dramatic or musical, every word or tone should be like a soldier marching towards the one common and final goal: the conquest of the material. Every fragment is impregnated with its mission toward this whole." Such is the focus of the "narration" of a tone poem. Tone poems are single-movement works.

Solo and Orchestral Piano Music

Les préludes (1854) is one of Liszt's most touching, spiritual works and is possibly one of the most popular symphonic tone poems ever written. The following words, taken from Lamartine's *Nouvelles méditations poetiques,* were printed in the score: "What is life but a series of Preludes to that unknown song of which death strikes the first solemn note?" Liszt advises that the Preludes are a series of emotional states that run the course of life and finally approach the unknown world lying at the close.

Mazeppa presents a rip-roaring wild horseback ride in which the horse carries the naked Ivan Stepanovich Mazeppa into the mountains as punishment for his affair with the wife of the Ukrainian king Casimir. The frenzied horse gallops through the score and suddenly (with a hideous musical shriek) collapses and dies. Mazeppa's music within the tone poem provides the thread of narrative or emotional continuity in the work. He survives the riding experience and ultimately triumphs to become the leader of the Cossacks. The work began as a piano piece and then was expanded to its tone poem format.

The two Piano Concerti (no. 1 in E-flat Major and no. 2 in A Major) are examples of Liszt's splendid writing for the instrument. Stirring orchestration, extravagant keyboard athleticism, gorgeous themes, and sparkling brilliance are hallmarks of both works.

Felix Mendelssohn (1809–47)

Amid the psychological turbulence and angst afflicting the lives of many nineteenth-century composers, Mendelssohn stands out as singularly happy and controlled, and could even be called well adjusted. In his compositions, Mendelssohn usually spoke in a cheerful, refined, well-trained voice. He remained immune to cosmic angst, neuroses, and deeply haunting moodiness which often motivated those around him. The composer had no revolutionary cause or deep message to broadcast. His music was usually relaxed, well crafted, poised, fluent, and lyrical. Mendelssohn was particularly famous for his fleet-footed, delicate writing: a splendid combination of presto (fast) pace with pianissimo (very quiet) dynamics. The result was enchanting music, seemingly free of gravity, soaring and spinning effortlessly. Mendelssohn was also known as a fine conductor and a promulgator of the music of J. S. Bach.

Overture to A Midsummer Night's Dream

When Mendelssohn was seventeen, he wrote a splendid overture which became an immediate hit and a signature piece for him. Originally the work was planned for two pianos but ultimately emerged in orchestral format. Mendelssohn captures the mood of the Shakespearean drama and evokes a supernatural, fairylike world in exquisitely delicate music which has cast its spell from that time to this. (This work is a splendid example of the fleet-footed, enchanting music mentioned in the introduction.) Years later, the composer added more incidental music to the drama.

Scottish *Symphony and* Italian *Symphony*

These two works are musical travelogues describing journeys which Mendelssohn had taken to the two countries. In both places he found inspiration from the landscapes and from their histories to write two

FIGURE 4.7. Mendelssohn, *A Midsummer Night's Dream,* excerpt.

of his most popular symphonies. Richard Wagner once observed that "Felix Mendelssohn" was a "landscape painter of the first order," a master in evoking a culture and a historical moment.

The *Scottish* Symphony came after his first visit to Scotland in 1829. (He visited Scotland nine times in his life.) On that first visit, he went to the site of Queen Mary's coronation. "Everything around is broken and moldering, and the night sky shines in ... I believe I found the beginning of my Scotch symphony there," the composer wrote. The symphony was published without the designation *Scottish*, however; this tag was added later. He was deeply moved by Scotland's atmosphere: the rocky coasts, the sturdiness of the people, and the intermittent fog. This symphony is the "serious Mendelssohn": evocative, captivating. The last movement is the most overtly Scottish sounding. The vigor of the music captures the energetic Highland fling and concludes in a brilliant coda.

The *Italian* Symphony was written in 1831. "This is Italy," he wrote. "What I have been looking forward to all my life as the greatest happiness is now begun and I am basking in it." The jolly mood, stimulated by the sunlit south, inspired one of his most happy works. He revised the symphony in 1838. The music continually reflects the joyful atmosphere with sparkling themes and colorful orchestration. The final movement references a sixteenth-century Italian dance called the *saltarello* and a visit to a Roman carnival where the composer had been pelted with sugar candies.

Olivier Messiaen (1908–92)

Olivier Messiaen was one of the most important composers, organists, and teachers of the twentieth century. His music offers one of the most intriguing voices of his time in its tender evocation of spiritual life and nature mixed with a profound emotion. Two sources basically shaped Messiaen's musical thinking: a profound religious faith (Catholic) and an abiding interest in ornithology. Regarding the first, he said, "The foremost idea I wanted to express in music, the one that is important because it stands above everything else, is the existence of the truths of the Catholic faith. . . . That is the first aspect of my work, the noblest, probably the most useful, the most valid, and the only one perhaps that I shall not regret at the hour of my death . . . I have tried to produce music that touches all things without ceasing to touch God." Regarding the second, Messiaen was an avid ornithologist, spending time in forests and jungles, listening to birds and writing down their songs and inflections. Often the direction "comme un oiseau" (like a bird) is written in his scores. (In The Technique of My Musical Language, Messiaen addresses his method of notating bird-song.) His mixture of modes (old scales) and complex rhythms (often serialized) animate much of his music in distinctive, unforgettable statements. "Bird pieces" include Oiseaux exotiques (wind, piano, and percussion) and Catalogue d'oiseaux (solo piano).

Quartet for the End of Time

The quartet was written in 1941, while Messiaen was held in a German prison camp, Stalag VIIIA. Using only the meager instruments available to him, Messiaen wrote one of the most stunning pieces of the twentieth century. Fellow musicians, who were also prisoners, performed the work for the entire camp of five thousand. The impact and promise of heavenly release were overwhelming, comforting, and sustaining when there was nothing left in the dire life of the camp. If you should desire to listen to a work of transcendent power, raw human emotion, and spiritual assurance spoken in twentieth-century musical language, this quartet is perfect. It is helpful to read the descriptions of each of the eight movements before you settle in for this extraordinary journey. If you ever have a chance to hear this work performed live, don't miss it!

Another piece not to miss is Vingt regards sur l'enfant Jesus (1944), a set of virtuosic piano pieces written for his second wife, Yvonne Loriod.

Wolfgang Amadeus Mozart (1756–91)

The great classical composer Wolfgang Amadeus Mozart burst on the musical scene as a child prodigy. By age eight he had written his first symphony, and his pianism was already extraordinary. During his short life, Mozart produced symphonies, concerti, operas, serenades, chamber music, and works for solo instruments of incredible beauty, grandeur, and imagination which have become timeless masterpieces.

FIGURE 4.8. Portrait of
Mozart. © Archivo
Iconografico, S.A./
CORBIS.

The identifying letter "K" refers to the chronological categorization
by Köchel. Sometimes Mozart's works are simply called "K. 430" or
"K. 478," for example.

The Serenades

Mozart's serenades are pieces written for celebrations and special
occasions. They are lighthearted, charming, and filled with ebullient
themes for diversion and entertainment.

His *Serenata notturno* is unusual in that it was written for two
orchestras, which were to be placed at opposite ends of a room,
resulting in a musical dialogue between the two ensembles.

The *Haffner Serenade* was written for the wedding of the daughter
of Sigmund Haffner (burgomaster of Salzburg), who was a friend of
the Mozart family. "It is in every sense of the word, a musical feast, in
which Mozart gives rein to his fancy," Saint-Fox observed. At all

times the music is celebratory, brilliant, and endlessly charming. There is also a *Haffner* Symphony (no. 35), which was commissioned by Herr Haffner for the ennoblement of his son.

The *Posthorn Serenade* is so called because of the inclusion of the instrument called a posthorn, which was used to announce the arrival of the mail as it was delivered to various towns on the mailman's route. There are several contrasting movements, before a concluding presto.

Eine kleine Nachtmusik (K. 525, A Little Night Music) is perhaps Mozart's best-known composition amid the serenades. It was written in 1787, the same year as his opera *Don Giovanni*. The beguiling music offers a first movement mini-sonata, a sentimental romanze, a poised minuet, and a bubbling rondo at the conclusion.

The Piano Concerti

Piano concerti are a major segment of Mozart's compositions. He wrote piano concerti throughout his life (there are approximately twenty-seven), and sometimes wrote them for his students and often for himself as soloist. In this genre, Mozart was not only a great innovator but also a stabilizer of the concerto form, establishing perfect balances between the soloist and the ensemble and distribution of thematic material. The concerti are diverse, colorful, and demanding in control and musicianship. K. 450, 453, 466, 467, and 503 will provide great pleasure for you in this genre.

The Symphonies

In the course of his life, Mozart wrote more than fifty symphonies. The first date from 1763–64 (when he was eighteen), and the last from 1788. Between 1764 and 1771 approximately thirty-five were written, between 1772 and 1781, approximately twenty-eight, and between 1782 and 1791, six.

SYMPHONY NO. 40

This symphony is singularly intriguing. Its pent-up energy and explicit emotional content separate it from the other symphonies. Richard Wagner called it "pivotal to the romantic world," a harbinger of things to come. The writing here is more personal than in the other symphonies, filled with chromaticism and turbulence. Mozart speaks very directly to us in this work, which is filled with passion and drama.

FIGURE 4.9. Mozart, *A Little Night Music*, K. 525, first movement.

SYMPHONY NO. 41 (*Jupiter*)

Standing at the crest of Mozart's symphonies, Jupiter can be viewed as a triumphant summation of his work in this field. It is not clear who provided the subtitle, but it appropriately suggests a certain other-worldliness and majesty. (Some have attributed the naming to J. B. Cramer.) Ironically, Mozart never heard this triumphant work played.

The optimism of the symphony contrasts mightily with the composer's personal circumstances. Financially, Mozart was in one of his many crises, and professionally, he was in an eclipse. Politically, Austria and the Ottoman Empire were fighting, and life was hard on everyone. The unbounded joy and power of this music triumphed over all such earthly adversity. Mozart was a genius at divorcing his music from his personal life, and in this case, we have a perfect example of that discipline and the dramatic power of his musical voice.

Modest Mussorgsky (1839–81)

The Russians have contributed greatly to Western music. Nationalist themes, imaginative orchestration, and intense lyricism are hallmarks of the Russian school. During the nineteenth century a particular set of Russian composers were known as "the Mighty Five," and Mussorgsky was one of those. Their mission was to cleanse Russian music of Western influences while defining and declaring a national sound.

Pictures at an Exhibition

Written in 1784, this suite began life as a piano work and was orchestrated later. In this vivid work Mussorgsky takes us to an art museum to view paintings and drawings by his friend Victor Hartman. As we stroll through the exhibit, Mussorgsky supplies "walking music." The pictures are varied, and the music captures each scene with great fidelity. Amid the selected pictures we find a gnome, a nutcracker, a ballet of chicks, two quarreling Jews, a marketplace filled with chattering housewives, catacombs, a surreal picture of a hut standing on chicken feet (the home of BabaYaga, the Russian witch), and a soaring ending describing the Great Gate of Kiev. The music is easy to follow because the composer provides the same strolling music (which opens the work) between the various scenes.

Night on Bare Mountain

This fantasy for orchestra describes a violent witches' Sabbath. The mountain referred to in the title is Mt. Triglav, near Kiev, which was (according to legend) inhabited by ghosts, witches, demons, and evil spirits and was governed by the black god, Tchernobog. Their horrendous party is depicted in stunning, evocative orchestration as we are taken into a supernatural world before church bells chime and dawn approaches, dispelling the frightening spirits.

Sergey Prokofiev (1891–1953)

The Prokofiev fingerprint is easy to identify: saucy, impudent, satiric, energetic, and surprising are words that all come to mind when describing his music. These were perhaps the most salient music features, yet

FIGURE 4.10. Sergey Prokofiev. © Bettmann/CORBIS.

looking at his work as a whole, the composer was indeed capable of moving away from iconoclastic behavior to write music of traditional beauties and sounds as well, such as his *Romeo and Juliet* ballet suites for orchestra.

Classical *Symphony*

Prokofiev's music was rarely mindful of tradition: from the beginning, his music tended to be shocking, bold, and defiant. But in his twenty-fifth year he decided to "write a symphony as Mozart or Haydn might have written it, had either one of them been a contemporary." The composer continued, "I christened it the Classical Symphony, first because it sounded much more simple and second out of pure mischief—to tease the geese—in secret hope that eventually the symphony would become a classic." The work premiered in Petrograd on April 21, 1918.

Mischief is everywhere in this lighthearted escapade. Mimicking the symphonic prototype of Haydn and Mozart, Prokofiev retains the classical forms but pours very different material into them. Spiky, nonlyrical melodics (sometimes sounding like wrong notes) replaced lyrical classical lines. Rhythms and harmonies are full of witty surprises as well, and throughout there is good humor and good times.

Second Piano Concerto in G Minor

"Music like this is enough to drive one out of one's mind." "It is a babble of insane sounds." "The cats on our roof make better sounds than that." These and worse opinions resulted after the premier of Prokofiev's Second Piano Concerto, in which the composer was the soloist. At the close, in spite of the hissing and booing, the composer defiantly approached the front of the stage and bowed—and further mocked the audience by playing an encore. Such behavior was typical of Prokofiev, a veritable enfant terrible who was never a compromiser. With great stamina and a certain belligerence, he maintained his own voice, and whether one liked him or not, he was impossible to ignore.

To our ears, it is strange that there were such wild reactions to his music. The nontraditional harmonies and surprising melodic shapes and behavior, which infuriated early audiences, merely sound fresh and witty, not the writings of a madman. The original score was lost in a fire, and in 1923 the concerto was rewritten. A ten-year interval separated the two premieres, and the second was with the Chicago Symphony on March 28, 1930, and again Prokofiev was soloist. One can only guess if he toned down any of the writing because as he aged, the composer became less experimental. In any case, the successor concerto was immediately acclaimed. Its brilliance, technical feats, and dramatic compass make this one of the most crowd-pleasing works in the repertoire.

Fifth Symphony

In 1944, after a fifteen-year hiatus in writing in the symphonic genre, Prokofiev wrote his Fifth Symphony. "I regard the Fifth Symphony as the culmination of a long period of my creative life. I conceived it as a symphony of the grandeur of the human spirit. The work is very important to me," the composer stated. The music is filled with folklike melodies, often cast in lower registers of the instruments, adding depth and richness. Its joy and optimism matched the mood of the day as Russians were celebrating the victory at Vistula. The first movement is filled with wonderful tunes and closes with an epic coda. Clarinets come forth in the second and third movement: in the first case, offering a perky, quirky theme over busy violin staccatos, and in the second case, calming the music to sing a soulful theme over throbbing strings. As the clarinet fades, critics believed that perhaps Prokofiev was recalling "the terrible price that the Russians were paying for their heroic resistance to the Nazi invaders."

Sergey Rachmaninoff (1873–1943)

Sergey Rachmaninoff was one of the most popular and affecting Russian composers of his time—and to this day. His heartfelt emotions pour into and out of his musical statements. Although Rachmaninoff lived until the midpoint of the twentieth century, he never was lured by "modernism" or the experimentalism which surrounded him. His was a voice richly imbued with the sounds, the language, and the passion of the romantic world.

Rachmaninoff explains, "I try to make my music speak simply and directly that which is in my heart at the time of my composing. . . . I compose music because I must give expression to my feelings, just as

I talk because I must give utterance to my thoughts." His deep humanity and willingness to share that humanity with us has resulted in some of the most compelling, magical music of the Western repertoire.

Second Symphony

The Second Symphony illustrates Rachmaninoff at full throttle. After the failure of his First Symphony, Rachmaninoff plunged into depression. Finally, the composer regained his composure, strength, and confidence (under the care of Dr. Nicholas Dahl, who also included some hypnosis and autosuggestion in his treatments) to address a symphonic idea again. The result was the enormous Second Symphony, which weighed in at 320 pages in the original manuscript. Herein you can find all the Rachmaninoff hallmarks: luscious melodies, boisterous dances, passionate introspective writing, emotional fervor, and bold, rich orchestration. Twenty-eight years were to pass before he tried his hand at another symphony.

The Piano Concerti

Rachmaninoff's three piano concerti are among the most famous and popular in the repertoire. The First has remained less played, although the composer revised it after moving to America. "It is really good now," he asserted. The fame of the other two constantly overrode the voice of the First.

The Second Piano Concerto was one of Rachmaninoff's most popular works and was played frequently on one of his American tours. Rachmaninoff noted that "these Americans cannot get enough of it." Themes from the concerto were extracted and became long-time favorites, such as the hit "Full Moon and Empty Arms," and the music appears in many film scores. The explanation for its popularity is simple: unforgettable melodies. "Melody is music and the foundation of all music. . . . I do not appreciate composers who abandon melody and harmony for an orgy of noises and dissonances," Rachmaninoff asserted. Indeed, this composer's hot-blooded style stood far apart from the mechanistic and severe attitudes driving many of his contemporaries.

Americans could not get enough of the Third Piano Concerto either. "My Third Piano Concerto was written especially for America," the composer stated. He also wanted money for a new car and had decided this work might provide the funds. Indeed it did. A brutal concert schedule, performing every day for three months, ensured the car purchase and also unveiled the concert twenty times across the continent.

From the opening, this concerto is a virtuosic vehicle for both ensemble and soloist. The vibrant display of pianism, unfettered orchestral power, rhapsodic themes, and unabashed, untempered emotions have made this work an enduring icon of romantic music at its best.

Maurice Ravel (1875–1937)

One of the most exquisite voices of the twentieth century was that of Maurice Ravel. Often coupled with Debussy as the "twins" of impressionism, Ravel's music differs in many ways from that of his compatriot. Precision, transparency, and objectivity are features of the Ravel style. "Where one shimmers, the other glitters," David Ewen explained.

Bolero

Unexpected notoriety came to *Bolero* when it was used as the background score for Dudley Moore and Bo Derek in the movie *Ten*. Concerning the piece *Bolero*, the composer wryly commented, "Alas, it contains no music!" Bolero is a compositional exploration of expressing a repeated melody without development. Tossed about the orchestra and into strange neighborhoods, such as high bassoon and tenor sax, the tune spins in a kaleidoscope of orchestral colors. Its massive statement at the conclusion requires thirty-six lines of score to formulate the full intensity! "I am particularly desirous there should be no misunderstanding about this work. It constitutes an experiment in a very special and limited direction and should not be suspected of aiming at achieving anything other or more than it actually does . . . it consists wholly of orchestra tissue, without music . . . and it is for the listeners to take it or leave it," Ravel stated to the *London Daily Telegraph* in 1931. Audiences have usually "taken it," and its extended crescendo and hypnotic nature has made it a hit in spite of the composer's "warnings."

Rapsodie Espagnole

Ravel's association with Spain was familial: his mother was Spanish and his childhood home had been near the Spanish border, where the Basque culture consistently flowed into France. Ravel was attracted to all things Spanish; Spanish inflections and sounds abound in his music. His *Habañera* (1895) became the basis of the third movement of the beautiful *Rapsodie espanole,* written in 1907. Also in that year he produced the beautiful *L'heure espagnole.* The music is filled with specific dances of Spain and evocative themes and orchestration, sweeping us to the Iberian peninsula.

La Valse

Ravel had served as an ambulance driver in World War I. After that experience, Ravel was unable to compose for two years: "the state of my health prevented me from working for some time. But when I started to compose again it was only to write *La Valse,* a choreographic poem."

Waltzing occupied a noted position in the opulent, sparkling world of the Viennese court. The romantic surges and lyrical content of the Viennese waltz seemed to symbolize a civilization of the highest order. The waltz emigrated from Vienna and became popular throughout Europe. Using the traditional Viennese waltz as a model, Ravel freely borrowed many of its features and effects. But he had in mind more than a copy. "I feel that this work is a kind of apotheosis of the Viennese waltz, linked in my mind with the impression of a fantastic wheel of destiny," the composer explained.

La Valse begins with a lovely scene (a huge ballroom lit by sparkling chandeliers). Spinning dancers grow more and more crazed as the waltz progresses on its destined course. Ingratiating waltzes and glorious climaxes occur in blazing orchestration, but the mood becomes steadily more sinister: the golden years of Vienna's splendor are at last turned into a sardonic judgment.

Ottorino Respighi (1879–1936)

Fountains of Rome

During his lifetime, Ottorino Respighi was one of the most successful and famous Italian composers of his generation. His resplendent three tone poems featuring Roman sights became international hits: *Fountains of Rome, Pines of Rome,* and *Festivals of Rome.* All are elegant, impressionistic pieces featuring exquisite melodies combined with descriptive components.

Fountains of Rome depicts four Roman fountains (those found at the Valle Giulia, Triton Fountain, Fountain of Trevi, and that of the Villa Medici) as they appeared at different times of day. *Pines of Rome* was inspired by the trees around the city itself, which are a significant feature of the city's landscape and character. Through the different movements, Respighi takes us to the "Pines of the Villa Borghese," the "Pines near a Catacomb," the "Pines of the Janiculum [Hill]," and the "Pines of the Appian Way." *Festivals* take us to the Circus Maximus, to a group of pilgrims who finally glimpse the city from Mount Mrio, from October celebrations, and from the eve of Epiphany in Piazza Navona.

Silvestre Revueltas (1899–1940)

Revueltas offers superb orchestral writing reflecting the music and culture of Mexico. His three tone poems for orchestra, y Cuauhnayhuac, Caminos, and Sensemaya, are excellent examples of a skilled composer evoking America's southern neighbor in vivid, charming, and exciting statements.

Nikolay Andreyevich Rimsky-Korsakov (1844–1908)

One of the most exciting members of the group known as the Mighty Five was Rimsky-Korsakov. His specialty was orchestration, and not only his writing but also a textbook attests to his excellence in the field. "Orchestration is the very essence of the composition. It is the birthright of every piece," he stated.

Russian Easter *Overture*

"The legendary and heathen side of the holiday, this transition from the gloomy and mysterious evening of Passion Saturday to the unbridled pagan religious merrymaking is what I was eager to reproduce in my overture," the composer explained. The sparkling piece premiered on December 3, 1888. It was one of the last orchestral works Rimsky-Korsakov wrote. In *My Musical Life* the composer noted, "These [the *Russian Easter* Overture and *Scheherazade*] close this period of my activity, at the end of which my orchestration had reached a considerable degree of virtuosity."

Scheherazade

In the eighteenth century, Europe was beguiled by the fantastic stories in *The Thousand and One Nights,* or *Arabian Nights.* For fourteen years, installments of these stories by Antoine Galland held a rapt audience. A stunning musical response came in Rimsky-Korsakov's four-part suite *Scheherazade,* composed in July 1888. Written the same year as *Russian Easter* Overture and based on the *Tales of the Arabian Nights, Scheherazade* was generated by one of the wives of the Sultan Schahriar, who had embarked on a bloody plan to execute his harem for assumed faithlessness. The brilliant (and buxom) Scheherazade managed to save her own skin by telling fanciful stories to her husband, who became so engrossed he spared her as long as her stories kept his interest. Ultimately, he abandoned the initial murderous plan. There are four glittery parts to the suite, and the voice of Scheherazade is throughout in triplet figures in solo violin.

Gioacchino Rossini (1792–1868)

Rossini is one of the most controversial composers of the nineteenth century. Sometimes labeled a major composer and at other times a fake and "mere tunesmith," the fact remains that he wrote engaging, saucy music at a time when Europe was in need of refreshment after the warring, intense Napoleonic Era. Personally, he was very likeable, a darling of the social circuit, and his devil-may-care attitude toward life was a social tonic. He disliked pedants and "heavy intellectuals." This aversion led him to create music which has a lighthearted, captivating nature. His operas focused on lighter plots and were simply a lot of fun.

He was a master of opera, and between 1815 and 1821 he penned sixteen operas. The overtures are spectacular examples of wit, fun, fluency, and the catchy tunes which were his signature statements. Italians were crazed with his style, and eventually Europe was also.

Fortunately, Rossini wrote at warp speed, churning out works at an incredible pace, because suddenly and inexplicably he retired at the height of his fame in 1829. From that time forward he was content to "hold his own court" in Paris.

Overture to The Barber of Seville

A famous example of Rossini's legendary speed was his composition of *The Barber of Seville*. During the time Rossini wrote this opera buffa, he never took the time to change out of his dressing gown. He never shaved either. "If I had shaved, I should have gone out. And, if I had gone out, I should not have come back in time to finish *The Barber* in thirteen days," he commented. The Overture is highly representative of the Rossini style, filled with rhythmic verve, rapid-fire motion, and brilliant tunes.

Overture to Semiramide

For this Overture Rossini uses the bright themes and tunes from the opera itself, much in the manner of a Broadway overture today. A brilliant close features the famed Rossini crescendo. In this event, the music enters a prolonged intensification, capped by an intoxicating orchestral roar. This technical thriller was a concert winner every time. Sometimes, because of his frequent use of this technique, Rossini was nicknamed "Signor Crescendo."

Camille Saint-Saëns (1835–1921)

From age three Camille Saint-Saëns composed, and continued to do so for the next eighty years. In addition to composing, he was said to write up to two dozen letters a day and was known also as a philosopher, an astronomer, and a poet, with side interests in drama and archeology. His music is poised, fluent, and always in refined taste.

Symphonic Poem: Phaëton

The musical narrative concerns Apollo's son, Phaëton, and his ill-fated effort to drive the chariot of the sun across the sky. Like a teenager who "borrows" the family car, Phaëton sets out on the ill-considered ride in the family chariot and predictably crashes. The tone poem is a vibrant rendering of the story, complete with a sad conclusion concerning Phaëton's foolishness in the coda.

Third Symphony (Organ)

Saint-Saëns's use of the organ in a symphony was unusual for its time, and hence the work is known as the *Organ* Symphony, although the organ part of the score is not virtuosic or soloistic. The symphony is written in two parts and is dedicated to Franz Liszt. The stirring nature of the music, the hefty rhythms, and the soaring lyricism result in a work which became one of the major concert favorites of its day—and today as well.

Concerto No. 2 for Piano and Orchestra

At the age of two Saint-Saëns was already creating tunes at the piano. He gave his first piano recital at age five. At age ten, at the esteemed Salle Pleyel, he was an immediate piano sensation.

His writing for piano and orchestra is exceptional in this concerto. The great pianist Arthur Rubinstein said, "for many years it served me as a first-rate warhorse. It has everything: dash, elegance, brilliance, and temperament. It is good music too! From beginning to end, this concerto is a virtuoso's dream come true!"

Carnival of the Animals

This work is subtitled *Zoological Fantasy*—and indeed it is. We are treated to lions, hens and roosters, donkeys, turtles, elephants, kangaroos, fish, birds, fossils, and a glorious swan. For fun, the composer added pianists as specimens of the zoo. Written for two pianos and orchestra, this humorous, glittering suite has been a concert favorite for children and adults since 1886, the year of its composition.

Arnold Schoenberg (1874–1951)

Schoenberg has been considered one of the most iconoclastic composers of the twentieth century. Often his name alone sends a shudder through concert audiences since he is indelibly linked to twelve-tone composition style, a method which resulted in a sound that is repelling and shocking to some and thrilling and refreshing to others. Irrespective of one's personal taste, it is important to acknowledge that far from being a defiant enfant terrible, Schoenberg's legacy deeply impacted the thinking and the sound of the twentieth century.

He did far more than attempt a fatal shot into the heart of Western music. His portentous musical pioneering began with the seemingly innocent belief that "Every tone relationship that has been used too often must finally be regarded as exhausted. It ceases to have power to convey a thought. Therefore, every composer is obliged to invent

FIGURE 4.11. Arnold Schoenberg in Los Angeles in the 1930s. Courtesy of the Arnold Schoenberg Center, Vienna.

anew." Despite the astonishing sound of his music, Schoenberg insisted, therefore, that his music was simply a continuation of the great German musical tradition, am evolution rather than a revolution.

Often criticized for being cold, inhuman, and cold-hearted, "like his music," Schoenberg responded later in his life, "if a composer does not write from the heart, he simply cannot produce good music. I get a musical idea for a composition. I try to develop a certain logical and beautiful conception and I try to clothe it in a type of music which exudes from me naturally and inevitably. I do not consciously create tonal, atonal, or polytonal music. I write what I feel in my heart, and what finally comes on paper is what first courses through every fiber of my body."

Arnold Schoenberg possessed more than a single twelve-tone voice, and if you are curious, consider the following. For a taste of twelve-tone music from the master: *Five Piano Pieces,* op. 23 (the concluding waltz); Suite for Piano, op. 25 (fully based on the twelve-tone system); *Variations for Orchestra,* op. 31; the opera *Moses and Aaron.* For a taste of his atonal, expressionist style: *Five Pieces for Orchestra.* For a taste of his more romantic style: *Verklarte Nacht* (chamber music version); the arrangement of the Brahms Piano Quartet in G Minor; *Theme and Variations for Orchestra,* op. 43b (in 1943 a band version of this work was completed).

Five Pieces for Orchestra

Schoenberg's *Five Pieces for Orchestra* premiered in 1912 with no movement titles. At first the work seemed confusing and chaotic, and Ernest Newman's review noted that the composer was "perhaps the only man in the world who knows what the music is intended to suggest." By 1922, Schoenberg revised many tempi and added titles to the movements, thereby clarifying meaning to some degree. In 1943 and 1973 *Five Pieces* was revised further, and the later version lists the following titles: "Premonitions," "Yesteryears," "Colors," "Perpetia," and "The Obligatory Recitative." *Five Pieces for Orchestra* has become one of the signature pieces of the twentieth century, with versions also for two pianos and for chamber orchestra.

Variations for Orchestra

This is a unique work for orchestra, utilizing Schoenberg's compositional method of twelve-tone music. This modern compositional technique sometimes rendered "bizarre" sounds and "strange" textures but, irrespective of its relative inaccessibility for general audiences, was a very significant exploration in the twentieth century's investigation of tonality and freeing music from the determinism of a tonal center. Thus, you will not find traditional, voice-based lyricism or easily recallable tunes in *Variations*. The determinism of the row (or theme) is controlling at all times.

Variations consists of an introduction, a theme, nine variations, and a finale, plus a later addition with an homage to J. S. Bach utilizing the German notation (B flat, A, C, B natural) in a four-note motive, recalling the letters of the name "Bach."

Franz Schubert (1797–1828)

In only thirty-one years, Franz Schubert bequeathed a musical legacy of enormous beauty. The composer was a sociable man who reveled in his friends and music. Whole evenings were sometimes devoted to his music at special parties called Schubertiads, in which Schubert performed for his loving fans. Songs, piano music, and sometimes chamber music occupied performers and guests until one or two in the morning. His love of people and of life is always reflected in his genteel, refined sound.

Most of all, Schubert is revered for his lyrical grace, and perhaps as a composer he was first and foremost a melodist. He wrote more than six hundred songs, which were grouped into sets known as cycles. That lyricism was a distinguishing characteristic of his symphonies, chamber works, and pieces for solo instruments.

Fifth Symphony

The Fifth Symphony was almost lost to us. Thanks to the work of Sir Arthur Sullivan and Sir George Grove, who were combing Vienna for lost Schubert manuscripts, the Fifth Symphony emerged. The first public performance took place fifty-seven years after its creation, at London's Crystal Palace on February 1, 1873. The form is classical, and the content is filled with the enchanting lyricism and emotion of early romanticism.

Eighth Symphony (Unfinished)

The nickname *Unfinished* attached to Schubert's Eighth Symphony could lead to an assumption that Schubert died while composing the work. In fact, he lived several years after the completion of the two movements which comprise this symphony. In the corpus of Schubert's works there are, in fact, six unfinished symphonies, of which this is the fourth. It was created in 1822 but was not premiered until forty-three years after its completion. Ironically, this symphony, which is one of the works most intimately identified with the composer, was one which he never heard played. The first movement opens with a poignant theme stated by celli and double basses. Soon the oboe and clarinet join in for a melancholy duet over pulsing strings. Simplicity and reticence seem to be the hallmarks of the idea; no hint is given of the fiery climax to emerge. The second movement opens calmly, like the first, with gently groping themes. In this we hear Schubert's skill in coloring his melodies with subtle harmonic shifts. Like the first movement, this one is also whipped into an emotional bonfire.

Symphony in C Major

Like the Fifth Symphony, this work could have been lost. In this case it was Robert Schumann who unearthed the manuscript by persuading Schubert's brother to allow him to peruse a stack of the composer's works. The entire C-major Symphony lay in the papers. Schumann seized the manuscript, dated March 1828, and sent it to be printed. As in the case of the preceding symphony, Schubert never heard this work performed.

Schumann reviewed the first concert (with Mendelssohn conducting) and wrote, "In Schubert's symphony, in the transparent glowing romantic life therein reflected, I see Vienna more clearly mirrored than ever before. Here we have besides masterly power over the musical technicalities of composition, life in all its phases, and permeating the whole work a spirit of romance." Other contemporary reactions were not as sympathetic, and it took years for the symphony to earn its rightful place in the standard symphonic repertoire.

William Schuman (1910–92)

Three Pieces for Orchestra 1956

By mid–twentieth century, the American musical scene was bursting with activity. An indigenous artistic base had formed in the New World that was not derivative of European models. It was a heady time. The United States could boast a long string of outstanding world-class composers: Copland, Piston, Barber, Ives, Dello Joio, Kirchner, Sessions, and William Schuman.

William Schuman was noted for his intriguing harmonies and imaginative rhythms. His "Americanism" is constantly revealed in the energy, liveliness, and daring found in his music, and he was inspired (some say preoccupied) with American sources. His opera *The Mighty Casey* was inspired by baseball, America's national pastime. *Three Pieces for Orchestra* was based on three tunes drawn from selected choral works by the American William Billings (1746–1800) and scenes from New England.

Robert Schumann (1810–56)

Robert Schumann was one of the greatest musical and literary voices of the nineteenth century. Outside of music, life was very difficult for Robert Schumann. Probably today he would be diagnosed with bipolar depression: his life was a series of highs and lows, and eventually, after several suicide attempts, he lived his final years in an asylum.

In 1841 Schumann turned his attention to writing for orchestra, having written primarily for piano up until that point. His four symphonies are exemplary documents of mid-century romantic taste and sensibility.

The First Symphony is called Spring and was written shortly after his marriage to Clara Wieck, a long-hoped-for event. The optimism and joy he felt in this event permeates the music.

The Second Symphony was written at a time when the "highs" from the marriage began to wear off. In 1844 he had a full nervous breakdown, and the Schumanns moved to Dresden for a quieter pace and lifestyle. The work was started in 1845, but with bouts of exhaustion and exuberance, he worked in fits and starts, trying to rest from the incessant ringing and roaring in his head. "The symphony is a souvenir of a dark period," Schumann recounted. (In fact, this should be the Third Symphony: the so-called Fourth was written second in terms of composition but was labeled the Fourth because of the order of publication.)

The Third Symphony, subtitled Rhenish, reflects Schumann's joy in being in the Rhineland and in Dresden. "Perhaps this mirrors here and there something of Rhenish life," he wrote to his publisher. High spirits animated the music—and this is one of the last interludes where optimism and joy enter into his music. But the optimism Schumann felt dissipated after this time. In only two years Schumann was asked to resign the music director's post of the Düsseldorf Orchestra.

In 1841, Schumann completed his D-minor Symphony. However, the work was withdrawn for ten years while Schumann wrote two more symphonies and did extensive revisions to the Fourth Symphony. These revisions concerned reorchestration of winds, and the pruning of thematic development. It premiered in Düsseldorf on March 3, 1853, with the composer conducting.

Schumann wanted a very unified work, and he decreed that all movements be played without pause. Further tightening the connectivity, Schumann used the same or derivative thematic material for all the sections. The first part opens with a tender melody (said to be a musical portrait of his wife), and shortly thereafter an arpeggiated figure is sounded which serves as a "motto" emerging throughout the work. Clara's theme and the motto surface repeatedly in all the sections before the exuberant finale. Donald Tovey noted that this "is perhaps Schumann's highest achievement for originality of form and concentration of material."

Dmitry Shostakovich (1906–75)

Amid all the political turbulence of his life, Shostakovich found time to author extraordinary symphonies, concerti, chamber works, and movie music. Perhaps no other composer in history has been so rocked by political acclaim and damnation. At one point in his life, Shostakovich kept a packed suitcase under his bed at all times in case he was suddenly whisked off to prison. At times he was the government's darling; at other times he was the icon of bourgeois Western decadence. "Following his music is difficult; remembering it is impossible. The danger of this trend to Soviet music is clear," Stalin commented in 1936.

The composer's resiliency amid these tormenting experiences was amazing. At times he would "comply" with the government, making public apologies and promising to write as the Communist Committee determined proper.

After 1948, the year of Stalin's death, government artistic controls were loosened somewhat. Shostakovich became freer to write without fear and within his stunning musical voice, although working under the Communist system posed the constant threat of censorship.

Fifth Symphony

Shostakovich's Fifth Symphony was issued ostensibly as an "apology" to the government for straying from the doctrines of Soviet realism. Its subtitle reads, *A Soviet Artist's Reply to Just Criticism.* Political artistic considerations involved rules such as writing folklike melodies, uncomplicated rhythms, and with a nonintellectual, nonpersonal attitude. Music was to be simple (perhaps mindless?) and accessible on an easy and large scale. The government's condemnation of Shostakovich occurred like a cycle: over and over again, with many "rehabs" to correct his errant musical behavior, which was considered traitorous.

The joke was that this symphony was in fact more intellectual, more personal, and more provocative than the preceding one, which had provoked both the punishment and the apology. Shostakovich in no way had capitulated from an artistic point of view, and the music pulled no punches. After the success of the First Symphony and the relative "failures" of the next three, the Fifth revived confidence in his ability to write meaningfully in the gigantic symphonic form. After the Fifth's premier, the *New York Times* wrote, "Composer Regains His Place in Soviet Music. Dmitry Shostakovich Who Fell from Grace Two Years Ago on Way to Rehabilitation, His New Symphony Hailed."

The Gadfly Suite

Shostakovich wrote movie scores for thirty-four movies (mostly of a political nature) during his career. *The Gadfly Suite* is one of his most famous and representative.

Jean Sibelius (1865–1957)

Jean Sibelius was one of the great Nordic composers to emerge in the late nineteenth and twentieth century. His personal focus and inspiration was his native Finland. Expressing the sound and the soul of Finnish culture was a lifelong mission for the composer. He became, however, far more than a fervent nationalist. His symphonies rank among the finest in the repertoire, moving his early musical orientation from the Finnish world to the international stage.

Finlandia

In 1899, responding to the issuance of the February Manifesto, which suppressed free speech and the press in Finland, Sibelius fought back against the Russians by writing a famous suite titled *Finland Awakes*. The fourth movement, divorced from the suite, was known simply as *Finlandia*. This stirring music became a rallying cry for Finnish patriots, and that patriotic current became so strong that the Russian government even issued a ban on *Finlandia*'s performance. *Finlandia* is a stirring, exciting, revealing work—and although people think Sibelius was quoting many Finnish folk tunes, he created all the themes himself.

Fifth Symphony

The Fifth is one of Sibelius's most impassioned, potent, and stirring works. Its optimism and power belie the frightening times in which it was written, during World War II. Karl Ekman wrote, "this is an expression of the creator's unshakeable faith in the ever-renewing power of life." Shattering climaxes, soaring themes, and intense passion reside in an unforgettable music which has never lost its power to thrill, captivate, and invigorate its audience.

Johann Strauss Jr., "the Waltz King" (1825–99)

Following in his father's footsteps, Strauss the Younger built a whole career on the waltz craze, which had become a European mania during the nineteenth century. Infectious, dazzling waltz tunes were enormously captivating and, quite simply, made people happy. Ballrooms throughout Europe (especially in Vienna) were filled with a dancing public, and no one served the dancers better than the Strauss family. (At one point Strauss Jr. opened a rival waltz orchestra to that of his father, but there was indeed room for both. Upon his father's death, he merged both ensembles.) *Tales from the Vienna Woods*, the *Blue Danube*, and *Wine, Women and Song* are typical examples of the orchestrated, buoyant, and irresistible dance music.

Richard Strauss (1864–1949)

Richard Strauss was a specialist in writing tone poems, large flexible structures (first generated by Liszt) in which a story or an extramusical idea is communicated. Strauss's efforts in this field at first led to some startling reactions. "An hour of music in an asylum," Debussy commented. "I find it a legitimate artistic method," Strauss maintained. Fortunately, the rest of the world seems to have agreed with Strauss and to have found these very unique works to be marvelous, enticing, and eminently transporting. Strauss moved far beyond communicating a musical story in a play-by-play narration. The music penetrates the mysteries of human motivations and psychology as well. Among his most famous tone poems are *Don Quixote* and *Thus Spake Zarathustra*.

Don Quixote

In October 1921, Strauss visited New York City. At that time he was asked, "what is your favorite symphonic poem?" He replied without hesitation, "*Don Quixote*." The setting of the classic Spanish novel by Cervantes went far beyond the usual descriptive method of program writing. In this remarkable setting, Strauss's music also depicts psychological changes of mind and psychological states (see fig. 3.18 for an excerpt). Muted instruments or a wandering melodic behavior reflect mental confusion, for example.

Don Quixote is played without pause and contains stunning effects. "Attacking geese" squeal through the orchestra in unmistakable bird-quarreling writing; the "Ride through the Air" incorporates the famous wind machine, and the depiction of the "errant knight's" character through the cello's voice takes us on a human experience which is both funny and deeply touching.

Thus Spake Zarathustra

If you saw Stanley Kubrick's *2001: A Space Odyssey,* the roaring opening theme that whirls the audience into space is quoted directly from Strauss's tone poem *Thus Spake Zarathustra.* Zarathustra, or Zoroaster, was an ancient seer, dating from the sixth century B.C., who had declaimed a set of pronouncements for mankind which would improve his character. The goal was ultimately to become an *Übermensch* (a superman). Structurally, there is an introduction and eight parts, all flowing into one another in a single movement. The composer's program notes for the premier state: "I wished to convey by means of music an idea of the human race from its origin, through the various phases of its development, religious and scientific, up to Nietzsche's idea of the superman."

Salomé

Strauss wrote in other forms besides tone poems, and one of his most sensual, unforgettable compositions is "The Dance of the Seven Veils," taken from his opera *Salomé* (1905).

Salomé's subject matter was, at best, controversial and was most often considered lurid and immoral. "The stench of Oscar Wilde's play [which provided the storyline, or libretto, for the opera] filled the nostrils of humanity," the *New York Times* sniffed. Another critic claimed, "and the music added to the degradation." Some opera houses refused to produce the opera "on moral grounds," but the premier in Dresden on December 9, 1905, was a wild success. Strauss, it was said, took twenty-five curtain calls.

The great climax arrives in "The Dance of the Seven Veils": a compendium of operatic themes and orgiastic thrills in which Salome provocatively dances for her lusting stepfather, King Herod. Slowly, steadily, she whips herself and the king into a frenzy, swirling and deviling herself. Incest, physical desire, and sex all combine in an extraordinary "unveiling" of emotions. Strauss remained immune to the moral challenges of *Salomé.* "I don't know what I am supposed to be redeemed from," Strauss insisted. He knew human nature and its components very well.

Igor Stravinsky (1882–1971)

Stravinsky was one of the most original, powerful, and influential composers of the twentieth century. His writing took many roads, and it is impossible to corral Stravinsky in a single definition.

In his early days, he drew musical inspiration from nationalist sources in Russian culture and history. At that time, Stravinsky wrote in a relatively conventional style.

Then, his voice trumpeted the "music of the future" in a revolutionary turnabout. In this phase rhythm became "liberated" from its corseted past. Suddenly, we find unusual units of seven or even thirteen beats. Accents shift capriciously. Percussion instruments march to the fore. In harmony, we find new discordant sounds thrust upon our ears, and melodies of the "old nature" seem to have shattered into short, often aggressive fragments.

In a subsequent phase, Stravinsky turned to a neoclassical style in which he invoked the structures and sounds of the past as an artistic compass. Later in the 1950s he had an avant-garde flirtation, writing twelve-tone music and serial music as well.

FIGURE 4.12. Igor Stravinsky. © Hulton-Deutsch Collection/CORBIS.

The Rite of Spring

Perhaps nowhere in the history of music was there such a violent reaction as that which ensued after the premier of Stravinsky's ballet *The Rite of Spring* (see fig. 3.21 for an excerpt). The story, set in pagan Russia, centers on the choosing of a young virgin (known as "the chosen") to sacrifice for the gods of spring to ensure fertility and a good harvest. The rite of spring refers not only to this matter of divine appeasement but also to the rites associated with annual ceremonies, dances, games, and events celebrating the earth and the breaking of the long Russian winter.

Stravinsky's music more than matched the primitive nature of the topic. Barbaric dances and "wild" orchestral statements unleashed music and scenes unlike any other. Stravinsky was well aware of the iconoclastic nature of the score, saying, "I was guided by no system whatever in *The Rite of Spring*." Then he added, "Very little immediate tradition lies behind it. I am the vessel through which The Rite passed."

Melodic, hypnotic repetitions, dominating, thumping, intrusive rhythms, and savage harmonies created tensions and sounds hitherto unheard, unexpected, and (at that time) deemed "intolerable." Even during the first performance the audience members could not wait until the ending to roar their disapproval. Early on in the premier, through hissing, foot stamping, and tomato tossing, they sent a furious commentary. The conductor, Pierre Monteux, remained "cool as a crocodile," according to Stravinsky, and somehow managed amid the fighting and flashing house lights to continue until the end of the score.

The passage of time has calmed the waters, and Stravinsky's brilliant score is respected and even venerated by some. Outside of the concert hall you can hear part of *The Rite of Spring*'s music in Walt Disney's classic 1938 movie *Fantasia,* which had a significant role in popularizing the music.

Petrushka

Petrushka was composed in 1911. This ballet was based on the unhappy little puppet Petrushka, who was well known to European fair goers. Stravinsky's music tells the story of Petrushka's ill-fated love affair, his fight with the burly Moor, and his final spiritual survival as a little ghost atop the roof of the little theater. The music reveals Stravinsky at his most captivating, innovative, and charming.

Concerto for Chamber Orchestra (Dumbarton Oaks)

This charming concerto is reminiscent of the old baroque concerto grosso style and was written to celebrate the thirtieth wedding anniversary of Mr. and Mrs. Robert Bliss, who lived at Dumbarton Oaks, Washington, D.C. In their honor, Stravinsky wrote the piece and titled it after their home. The clean, disciplined, glittering writing stands in sharp contrast to the explosion of *The Rite of Spring* and the folkloric coloration of *Petrushka*. Stravinsky was now in his neoclassic phase, and this work is a fine specimen of that phase. "I do not think that Bach would have begrudged me the loan of these ideas and materials, as borrowing in this was something he liked to do himself," Stravinsky commented when his attention was brought to the fact that one of the concerto's themes suspiciously resembled one of Bach's (used in a *Brandenburg* Concerto).

At the time of this writing, Stravinsky was visiting the United States (for the third time) and was considering moving to America, which he did in 1940, to make his home in Hollywood. Not only did Southern California offer alluring weather (helpful to the tuberculosis which ran through his family), but it also provided a haven from the impending war.

"Star-Spangled Banner"

After settling in America in 1940, Stravinsky reharmonized the "Star-Spangled Banner." This was done as a "vehicle," through which, as Stravinsky states, "I might best express my gratitude at the prospect of becoming an American citizen." Later he wrote to a friend that he hoped that Congress "will pass an act standardizing my harmonization," but that still remains unlikely to happen. In any case, it is an interesting experience to hear the thoughts of the great composer underpinning this very familiar tune.

Pyotr Ilyich Tchaikovsky (1840–93)

Most of us recognize Tchaikovsky's music through the Christmas-time favorite *The Nutcracker* (see fig. 4.13 for an excerpt). Many of his signature traits are found in this score: lush themes, imaginative orchestration, and intense personal emotions.

Sixth Symphony (Pathetique)

One of Tchaikovsky's most intense musical statements is his Sixth Symphony, which the composer premiered only a few days before his death. The subtitle is from the Russian word, meaning a large emotional experience rather than the English cognate "pathetic." Traditional Tchaikovsky melancholy permeates the work, but enormous power and personality are invested in music of unrelenting emotional eloquence.

Romeo and Juliet *Overture*

To many, this is the most powerful love music ever written. The reviewer Kern Holomon wrote, "It is quite simply the best love music there is." The famous love theme pervades the whole overture, placed in different areas of the orchestra and presented in varying styles. Tchaikovsky teases us by delaying its most expanded articulation, letting the theme begin modestly and grow to the heated, sensuous climax.

In late 1869, Tchaikovsky attended *Romeo and Juliet,* and his enthusiasm for the play (and for the lovely singer Desirée Artot) was the inspiring source for the overture. He "fell in love with her" and often fantasized about a union, despite his homosexuality. A vivid response to the score came from the composer Balakirev, who commented, "When I play this I visualize you wallowing [in] your bath with Artot, rubbing your stomach ardently with fragrant soap suds."

Violin Concerto

Tchaikovsky's Violin Concerto is one of the most popular ever written. Early negative opinions have long since vanished, and it is reliably a concert favorite. One of those reviews, by Eduard Hanslick, stated, "The violin is no longer played: it is yanked about, it is torn

FIGURE 4.13. Tchaikovsky, *The Nutcracker Suite*, "Dance of the Sugarplum Fairy."

asunder, it is beaten black and blue. I do not know whether it is possible for anyone to conquer these hair-raising difficulties."

The concerto is indeed filled with virtuosic writing, but hardly is the violin "torn asunder." Intensely lyrical themes and colorful orchestral partnership make this one of the most intimate and moving violin concerti in the repertoire.

Swan Lake *(Orchestral Suite)*

The suite is a selection of specific numbers gathered from the original thirty-three which were created for the ballet *Swan Lake.* Combining deep appreciation for the dance with his composing talent, Tchaikovsky raised ballet music from mere accompaniment to an independent genre. Sometimes the composer even called his music for ballet "dancing symphonies."

In 1875 Tchaikovsky accepted eight hundred rubles to write the ballet music for *Swan Lake.* "I accepted the work partly because I needed the money and because I have long cherished a desire to try my hand at this type of music." It was his first ballet score, and success came slowly. Ultimately, his music for ballet became so influential that Zhitmomirsky, an esteemed Russian critic of ballet music, observed that "Tchaikovsky created a fundamental change in the role of music in ballet. It almost always rises above the elements of the subject and stage of his ballets." In the case of *Swan Lake,* the beginning was not auspicious. At first the dancers complained that it was "undanceable," and the conductor thought the score was "too hard." To rectify this, he simply omitted two-thirds of the score in the ballet's premier. Eventually, the music was basically lost as the ballet faded from view.

In 1894–95 Marius Petipa revived both the ballet *Swan Lake* and Tchaikovsky's music to the stature and respect it still receives today.

Antonio Vivaldi (1678–1741)

Antonio Vivaldi was one of the most colorful, dramatic composers and violin performers of the baroque period. At one point he was listed as a "tourist attraction" in his native Vienna. He boasted bright red hair and was therefore called "the Red Priest" since his ordination in 1703 (see fig. 2.2 for a caricature of Vivaldi). Occasionally, music critics have deduced that his fiery music stemmed from his red hair.

For nearly forty years, Vivaldi was music director of the Pio Ospedale della Pieta, a famous Venetian conservatory orphanage serving parents who could not afford to bring up their children. There the girls were trained to excel in music. Vivaldi had a built-in site and a set of musicians for his compositions.

As a composer Vivaldi was especially noted for his concerto production. His output was prolific: 46 operas (at one point he became manager of the San Angelo Opera House), more than 60 sacred works, and 40 cantatas—as well as approximately 550 concerti, of many natures and combinations. He loved contrast in writing, and the concerto idea of placing a small group or solo instrument in contrast to the larger ensemble was intriguing to him. Instrumental coloration was an important feature in his writing, and he was one of the few Italian composers of his time who was interested in woodwind instruments. His experiments in antiphonal placement of instrumental groups within the cathedral yielded dramatic acoustical contrasts. To some his energetic, dramatic writing was overblown and frenzied, but significant composers such as J. S. Bach and Johann Quantz were staunch admirers of his style. Bach, in fact, transcribed some of the Vivaldi concerti for keyboard.

The Four Seasons

This set of four violin concerti was published in Amsterdam in 1725 as part of a larger collection called *Il cimento dell'armonia a del'invention* (The Contest of Harmony and Invention), written for Count Graf Wenzel von Morzin of Bohemia. Each of the four movements represents a season of the year, and Vivaldi included a personally written sonnet to describe the music. Further, just to make certain the performer didn't miss anything, he inserted words where the programmatic effects were occurring. Programmatic music was unusual at this time, and these concerti stood well outside the norm in that regard. Within the Vivaldi oeuvre there are only twenty-eight pieces which include titles. If you like these, there are hundreds more to sample from his gigantic output.

Specific descriptive musical inflections and textual influences are revealed in part by the following samples from the concerti. In "Spring," bird trills and a bright opening represent the happiness and excitement of spring. Watery effects in rocking violin phrases echo the sound of murmuring streams. In "Summer," the sonnet reads, "in the heat of the blazing Sun"; the music itself is enervated, exhausted. Birds emerge in fast fluttering leaps as "the cuckoo raises his voice and the turtle-dove and goldfinch join in the song." In "Autumn," the jolly opening orchestral section (called a ritornello) reflects the joy of a fine harvest, while "At dawn the hunters set out with horns, guns and dogs" (this is represented by a bright, energetic hunting theme, which also gives way to terrified animals in tremolos from the strings). In "Winter," the frozen world is represented by an almost motionless subject. "In the severe gusts of a terrible wind" we find racing scales in the violin solo, "running and stamping one's feet constantly" (repeated note).

The text and the music are closely related, and taking the time to read the text with the music will greatly enhance your experience and acquaintance with *The Four Seasons*.

Richard Wagner (1813–83)

Richard Wagner was one of the most influential, towering figures in the history of Western music. His innovations and influence were revolutionary, and some have said that he so dominated the second half of the nineteenth century that most of the music written therein was either an imitation or a reaction. He wrote thirteen gigantic operas and music dramas, assorted orchestral works, an oratorio, a piano sonata, and various influential texts, including *The Music of the Future, Opera and Drama, Religion and Art, Autobiography,* and *Conducting.* The composer reveled in the thought of leading a musical revolution, and his music dramas were experiments in synthesizing the arts into a form called *Gesamtkunstwerke.*

At all times, Wagner's music for the drama integrates with the plot, directly connecting to or commenting on the action or psychological states and emotions of the characters and events. The Wagner operas were filled with complicated plots and psychological and physical adventure and often included supernatural influences and fateful controls. His music is written on a lavish canvas, usually for huge orchestras, and is fully committed to "participation" rather than mere accompaniment to the events on stage. You do not really need to know the plot

Figure 4.14.
Richard and
Cosima Wagner.
Courtesy of the
Richard Wagner-
Stiftung, Bayreuth.

to enjoy the sweep and grandeur of Wagnerian overtures. His voice and talent are unmistakable, unforgettable, and transporting.

The composer's personal life was filled with controversy. In fact, no musician probably had more enemies or passionate disciples. On the one hand, he was a habitual adulterer, rabid anti-Semite, musical revolutionary, and political dissident. On that side of things he was reviled. "He has made music sick" and "He is a corrupter of the art" were common viewpoints. On the other hand, Wagner was beloved and was considered a hero, an inventor of a new musical language, and a voice of the future. His disciples were rabid in their praise and commitment. Wagnerites and anti-Wagnerites were clearly defined camps in the late nineteenth century.

"Ride of the Valkyries"

"Ride of the Valkyries" from *Die Walküre* is one of the most splendid examples of Wagner's magical orchestration. As the Valkyries (nine warrior maidens) ride their horses through the air, the orchestra accompanies them in music portraying the wind, the galloping horses, and the women's war cries.

Overture to The Flying Dutchman

Franz Liszt wrote that "This must be placed on a level of the best marine painters. No one has ever created a more masterly orchestral picture. . . . One feels tempted to exclaim it is wet!" Within his surging musical ocean, Wagner draws the tale of the Dutchman, cursed to wander the world in a ghost ship (complete with blood-red sails) and allowed to visit shore only once every seven years. Eventually, the love of a good woman (as in many of his operas) redeems the Dutchman, and the pair ascend to heaven as the ship sinks to a watery grave. Psychological references abound in Wagner's music for this drama, the first time this non-musical dimension was represented in his works. The overture was written in seven weeks during the summer of 1841.

A Siegfried Idyll

Wagner's music was not entirely bombastic and huge. One of his most endearing works is the tender *Siegfried Idyll*. On December 25, 1870, Cosima Wagner came downstairs to hear Wagner's Christmas and birthday gift to her—a tender lullaby known as *A Siegfried Idyll*. The full title referred to their baby son, Siegfried, who was also known as "Fidi." Hence the complete title reads "Tribschener [the name of their house was Tribschen—the *er* is a modifying ending] idyll, with Fidi's Birdsong and Orange Sunrise, as a symphonic Birthday greeting from Richard to Cosima."

Cosima's diary recorded the event, stating, "As I awoke my ear caught a sound, which swelled fuller and fuller; no longer could I imagine myself to be dreaming; music was sounding, and such music!" The orchestra was invited to stay for a glorious Christmas celebration. The piece was not intended for public hearing, but in later years, due to severe financial distress, Wagner was forced to sell the work. Besides the references made in the title, the work contained many references to deeply private matters between the couple.

A Final Note

In the twenty-first century, there is a growing, stellar set of American composers whose musical voices will certainly become classics in the history of music. A limited list includes Michael Torke, John Corigliano, Ellen Zwilich, Michael Daugherty, Christopher Rouse, Lowell Liebermann, Theodore Shapiro, Roberto Sierra, and Aaron Jay Kernis. Keep listening and looking for new masterworks that speak to you.

GLOSSARY

ABA form: a ternary structure in which the A section is followed by a contrasting B section and rounded out by a return of the A section

Accelerando: accelerate

Adagio: slow

Aleatoric: chance, random

Alla marcia: in a marching style

Allegro: happy in mood; for a tempo marking, means at a "cheerful pace"

Andante: from *andare* (to walk), at a moderate or walking pace

Arco: with the bow, as opposed to **pizzicato**

Aria: a song usually for voice, often written in **ABA form;** can also be an instrumental piece written in a songlike structure or feeling

Attaca: move immediately to the next movement without pause or separation

Beats: the steady heartbeat or pulse of the music

Cadenza: A section in a **concerto** when the soloist performs without ensemble; usually a virtuosic statement and vehicle for technical display

Cantabile: in a singing style

Chord: see **harmony**

Coda: from the Latin meaning "tail," a distinctive musical section attached at the end of a work or movement

Con: one of the most common modifiers, means "with"

Con allegrezza: with cheerfulness

Con brio: with spirit

Con fuoco: with fire

Concerto: a work featuring a solo instrument or group of instruments

Contrapuntal: written in a **polyphonic** style

Crescendo: growing louder gradually

Decrescendo: growing softer gradually

Diminuendo: growing softer gradually

Dolce: sweet

Dynamics: the louds and softs of the music

Espressivo: with expression and emotion

Fantasia or fantasy: a piece in free form, improvisatory in nature

Flat: lowers a specific note

Forte: loud, indicated by an "f"

Fugue: a **contrapuntal** form stemming from the baroque

Giocoso: playfully

Grave: very slow

Harmony: 1. combining different notes to be sounded simultaneously; the resulting combination is called a **chord**. 2. a set of rules, often very complex, governing the movement or progression of chords as well as the various combinations of tones used within the chord itself.

Homophonic: a single melodic line predominates

Instrumentation: see **orchestration**

Interval: the distance between two notes

Key signatures: a set of **flats** or **sharps** at the beginning of a piece which indicates the **scale** being used

Largo: slow

Legato: from the Italian verb *legare*, meaning to link; hence, the notes are connected and smooth

Lento: slow

Ma non troppo: but not too much

Maestoso: majestically

Major and minor: designates the intervallic pattern of the **scale** or key being used; for example, a C scale or the key of C can be either C major or C minor. Used almost exclusively in Western art music after the baroque period, replacing the **modes.**

Melody: a tune

Minor: see **major**

Moderato: at a slow, moderate pace

Modes: old forms of **scales** that sound different from basic **major/minor scales** because the **intervals** between the notes are arranged in a different pattern. Primarily heard in early music, but later composers also use modes to provide a special effect.

Modulate: moving to a different key or different **scale**

Molto: much, very

Morendo: dying away

Motif: a small, distinctive melodic fragment

Nocturne (notturno): a night piece, usually of a quiet nature

Opus: work

Orchestration: the process of choosing which instrument will play the music

Ostinato: a repeating pattern (of tones, harmonies, or rhythms) usually sounded in the bass

Overture: an opening piece derived from a dramatic source such as an opera; also a work written in the style of an opening piece

Piano: soft, indicated by a "p"

Piu: more (e.g., piu forte—louder)

Piu mosso: with more motion, faster

Pizzicato: plucking the string to produce a staccato sound

Poco: little (e.g., poco ritardando—slowing down a little)

Polyphonic: several musical lines sounding simultaneously

Portamento: notes are separated but not with the incisive touch of staccato

Presto: fast

Program music: music which is inspired by or based on an extramusical source such as literature or paintings

Quasi: almost, like

Rallentando: getting slower gradually

Recitative: in opera the declamatory style of singing (usually advancing the plot) as opposed to the **arias;** in instrumental music, means to play in a recitativo style, meaning in a declamatory nature

Rhythm: a pattern of accents working in combination with the **beats**

Ritard: slowing down (indicated by "rit")

Rondo: from the French *rondeau;* the initial theme recurs over and over with interpolated sections between the recurrences

Scale: successive notes of a fixed pattern of **intervals,** usually whole and half-steps

Serenades: also known as divertimenti; light-hearted music written for entertainment

Sforzando: a sudden accent, indicated by "sfz"

Sharp: raises a specific note

Sonata-allegro form: a tripartite structure highly developed in the classical period and used in the ensuing centuries; most often used in the first movement of **symphonies** or sonatas, although it is subject to hybrid formations as well, such as sonata-rondo

Sonatina: a small sonata

Sotto voce: quietly

Staccato: separated notes, not connected

Subito: suddenly

Subject or theme: the main tune or melody of a composition: usually called a subject in a **fugue** and a theme in **sonata form**

Suite: a set of dances or dancelike music

Symphony: a three- or four-movement orchestral work, generally employing **sonata** form

Tempo: the speed of a piece

Theme: see **subject**

Time signatures: a combination of numbers stacked horizontally appearing at the beginning of the staff after the clef

Toccata: from *toccare,* to touch; usually a keyboard work which is virtuosic in nature

Tone poem: see **program music**

Variations: a form of music in which a **theme** is presented and various sections follow with variations on the theme

Vibrato: alternating the pitch of a voice or instrument to add greater warmth to the sound

Vivace: lively, with life

INDEX

Italicized page numbers indicate illustrations.

MARIANNÈ WILLIAMS TOBIAS is a cum laude graduate of Harvard University, Longy School of Music, and the University of Minnesota, where she earned an M.F.A. and a D.M.A. A seasoned pianist, public radio commentator, lecturer, and writer, Tobias is known for her crisp, engaging style and lively narration.